The Land Qu

The Land Question

Fixing the dysfunction at the root of
the housing crisis

Daniel Bentley

CIVITAS

First Published December 2017

© Civitas 2017
55 Tufton Street
London SW1P 3QL

email: books@civitas.org.uk

ISBN 978-1-906837-93-8

Independence: Civitas: Institute for the Study of Civil
Society is a registered educational charity (No. 1085494)
and a company limited by guarantee (No. 04023541).
Civitas is financed from a variety of private sources to
avoid over-reliance on any single or small group of donors.

All publications are independently refereed. All the
Institute's publications seek to further its objective of
promoting the advancement of learning. The views
expressed are those of the authors, not of the Institute.

Typeset by
Typetechnique

Printed in Great Britain by
4edge Limited, Essex

Land is limited in quantity while the demand for it, in a prosperous country, is constantly increasing. The rent, therefore, and the price, which depends on the rent, progressively rises, not through the exertion or expenditure of the owner, to which we should not object, but by the mere growth of wealth and population. The incomes of landowners are rising while they are sleeping, through the general prosperity produced by the labour and outlay of other people.

John Stuart Mill, 1871

Author

Daniel Bentley is editorial director at Civitas, where he has worked since 2013. Prior to that he was political correspondent at the Press Association. His previous housing papers include 'Finding Shelter: Overseas investment in the UK housing market' (with David Green, 2014), 'The Future of Private Renting: Shaping a fairer market for tenants and taxpayers' (2015), 'The Housing Question: Overcoming the shortage of homes' (2016) and 'Building Homes Faster? A commentary on the government's plans for increasing the pace of development' (2017).

Acknowledgements

I am very grateful for invaluable comments on earlier drafts from Thomas Aubrey, Richard Blyth, Peter Saunders and Anastasia de Waal. All of the views expressed and any errors are of course mine alone.

Contents

Summary

There is a widespread consensus that we need to build more homes. The challenge, however, is not just to raise total output but to ensure that the right types of housing are delivered and in the places they are needed most. The current housebuilding framework has shown itself to be not up to the task. Total housing supply has, on most accounts, been insufficient for the levels of population growth and household formation the country has experienced and is forecast to experience in the years ahead. Meanwhile, the provision of affordable and sub-market housing is being increasingly squeezed out by the development process. There is much regional variation, however, and these shortfalls are most acute in the fastest-growing areas that are experiencing the greatest increases in demand and the highest housing costs.

It is argued here that, while there are various factors at play, the root of these problems lies in the trade in land. Large fortunes can be and are being made out of the sale of development land for new housing, particularly in those areas – notably London and the South-East – where prices have risen the most. But the pursuit by landowners of the highest-value developments for their sites is frequently at odds with the delivery of more affordable homes and speedier construction. It also leads them to withhold sites from the development process, possibly for many years, while they wait for prices to rise and more profitable schemes to emerge. When a deal is finally struck and land is released for construction, the development will usually be targeted at the more expensive sections of the market. Housing developments of any size will be built slowly, over many years, because the developer must maintain the value of the land so that they are able to pass it on to their customers in the price of a new-build home. Commitments to affordable housing provision as a condition of development may be revised down if the price that has been paid for the land is felt to be incompatible with their delivery.

It is for these reasons that simply releasing more land for development in the highest-demand areas will not on its own overcome the problems that the housing market currently faces. Landowners, in possession of a geographical monopoly, have a power of constraint over the development priorities of the community. In high-value areas and rising markets they are especially incentivised to drip-feed new residential land over an extended period of time. This feature of the land market is of long-standing, having been observed in many different housing markets and at many different points in history. It predates the 1947 planning system and the introduction of the green belt. Reform of planning to ensure more land is made available for development is important, but it must be accompanied by new incentives for landowners to part with sites sooner and at lower prices that are compatible with planning objectives.

The key to this lies in reform of the Land Compensation Act of 1961, which enshrines in law the right of landowners – in the case of compulsory purchase by the state – to be reimbursed not only for the value of their site in its current use but for any prospective use to which it might be put in the future. Their entitlement to this 'hope value' means public authorities are powerless to enforce development priorities that are in the interests of the community. This was not always the case: the new towns that were initiated before the 1961 Act, and much of the local-authority output of the late 1940s and 1950s, was underpinned by a land-values policy that meant landowners were compensated at values reflecting the existing use of the site. This meant land for new homes could be acquired at or close to its much lower agricultural or industrial use values. It also doused speculation and prevented the withholding of land.

Revising the 1961 Act, so that assessments of market value do not incorporate prospective planning permissions, would reframe incentives in the land market by enabling public authorities to acquire development sites at prices closer to its existing use value. This would have a cascade of benefits for housebuilding. By taking away from landowners their entitlement to speculative values, it would remove the incentive to hold out for aspirational prices. This would enable developers to get hold of land at prices that are compatible with planning obligations, the provision of more affordable homes and quicker build rates. It would also make it much easier and much cheaper to embark on a new generation of council housebuilding and/or a new programme of new towns and garden villages.

This is not just a simple change in the law. It raises important questions about property ownership and the balance between the rights of the private landowner and the rights of the wider community. It calls for a reconsideration of attitudes to land ownership and of what landowners' rights should, and should not, encompass. Specifically, it requires policymakers to accept what the classical economists argued but which is largely forgotten today:

that increases in locational land values are an 'unearned increment', generated not by the owner of the land but by the labour and the investments of the community.

Introduction

On July 17th, 1909, a crowd of about 3,000 people gathered at the King's Theatre in Edinburgh to hear a speech by a young Liberal MP by the name of Winston Churchill. He was there to promote the 'People's Budget' that had been presented to parliament a few months earlier by David Lloyd George, and in particular the controversial measures in it to tax land. Churchill, then 34 but already president of the Board of Trade, asked the audience to imagine an unused plot of land in one of the country's growing cities. The landowner 'sits still and does nothing' while around his plot the population makes the city larger, more prosperous and more convenient:

> Roads are made, streets are made, railway services are improved, electric light turns night into day, electric trams glide swiftly to and fro, water is brought from reservoirs a hundred miles off in the mountains – and all the while the landlord sits still. Every one of those improvements is effected by the labour and at the cost of other people. Many of the most important are effected at the cost of the municipality and of the ratepayers. To not one of those improvements does the land monopolist as a land monopolist contribute, and yet by every one of them the value of his land is sensibly enhanced. He renders no service to the community, he contributes nothing to the general welfare; he contributes nothing even to the process from which his own enrichment is derived.

If the land were occupied by shops or by dwellings, the municipality at least would secure the rates upon them in aid of the general fund, but the land may be unoccupied, undeveloped, it may be what is called 'ripening' – ripening at the expense of the whole city, of the whole country, for the unearned increment of its owner.[1]

No taxes are being collected from the plot of land because it is not in use. Those improvements that are raising the value of it are being funded by those living in the area and engaging in productive activity. But while the land is kept in a state of disuse, the city around it is getting more congested, housing accommodation is becoming more costly and overcrowded, and the value of the plot is rising until, finally, the price 'is too tempting to be resisted any longer':

Then, and not till then, it is sold by the yard or by the inch at ten times, or twenty times, or even fifty times its agricultural value, on which alone hitherto it has been rated for the public service. The greater the population around the land, the greater the injury which they have sustained by its protracted denial, the more inconvenience which has been caused to everybody, the more serious the loss in economic strength and activity, the larger will be the profit of the landlord when the sale is finally accomplished.[2]

Churchill's cri de coeur against the privileges of the free-riding land monopolist followed the contours of a debate that had been unfolding for more than a century, and had become increasingly more relevant as industrialisation and urbanisation progressed through the nineteenth century. The land question could be traced back through the works of the classical economists to Adam Smith, who identified rent – the return to land – as a monopoly price, 'naturally the highest which the tenant can afford to pay'.[3]

It is now just over a century since Churchill's Edinburgh speech, and the issue he was addressing has not been resolved. The ability of a landowner to hold out for values they have not themself created, and in doing so create a hindrance to development, lies in many respects at the root of the housing difficulties policymakers are grappling with today. As I will set out in the following chapters, this amounts to a power of constraint, above and beyond any constraints imposed by the planning system, that needs to be overcome.

There are two central aspects to this. The first is the ability of the owner of potential development land to hold out indefinitely for an aspirational price, a problem that is amplified further in a market that only ever seems to rise. This means that land for new residential development is slowly drip-fed at prices that are often on the margins of what the market can absorb, slowing down housebuilding and skewing development priorities away from affordable homes. The second is the right of the landowner to collect most of the capital value that is realised when a sale is finally made, even though that value has been generated by the investments and enterprise of the surrounding community. This is an encouragement to the landowner to withhold their plot, but it is also a financial loss to the community. Moreover, if the community wishes to buy land for its own purposes – for example, to build social housing – it must reimburse the owner for the value that it has already created.

This has generated vast windfalls for landowners. When we think about high house prices what is really meant is high residential land prices. It is not the value of the bricks and mortar of our homes that has appreciated so much in recent decades, nor the labour costs of constructing them, but the plot of land on which they sit. It is estimated that

74 per cent of the increase in UK house prices between 1950 and 2012 was due to land price inflation.[4] Most of that increase has taken place since the mid-1990s, when house prices began to accelerate at unprecedented speed. Between 1994 and the financial crisis of 2007, land in England with residential planning permission almost quadrupled in real-terms, from an average of £1.3m a hectare to just over £5m a hectare (in 2016 prices).[5]

The windfall comes when a piece of land undergoes a change of use from agricultural or industrial to residential. A hectare of land is worth on average about 100 times as much when it is used for housing than it is when it used for farming. Brownfield sites in industrial use will be worth more but the multiple when it is converted to residential can still be very large, depending on the location. In 2014/15, landowners collected more than £9 billion in profit from land they had sold for new housing.[6] This means that for each new home built that year, £60,000 on average went to the original landowner (or was shared between various landowners who may have traded it over a period of time prior to development). Such profits enjoyed by a relatively tiny number of people are the flipside of the housing affordability crisis we are grappling with today: the more house prices rise, the more landowners can command for sites suitable for new housing.

That landowners should automatically enjoy most of this increase in land values – what Churchill, and others, called the 'unearned increment' – has been largely taken for granted by policymakers for several decades. But it is time we questioned once more why that should be so. As policymakers try to find ways of improving the provision of housing – not just in terms of numbers, but in terms of quality, affordability and place-making – these are issues that need to be addressed once more. Not only is the community being deprived of the value it has created, but housing provision is being constrained because of the impact of land prices on housebuilding. The high cost of land increases the risk that developers must bear, limiting the rate at which new homes can be built, and means that state subsidies for affordable housing go a lot less further than they would have done in, say, the 1950s. High land prices are, in part, the consequence of a shortage of homes in the places we most need them – but they also place a brake on further supply and so are a cause of it too. The rising price of land generates its own positive feedback loop that only benefits those who own it.

Governments in the past, and elsewhere in the world to this day, have made various attempts to capture these land values for the common good. Such a framework underpinned the development from scratch of all of the post-1945 new towns, and was also used in the council building programmes of the 1940s and 1950s. If, like then, land for new housing could be purchased by the state at something closer to its existing use value, rather than its residential value, we could finally start to build more of the housing we need, where we need it most.

1

Housebuilding and the role of land

'Homebuilders deliver new homes as fast as they can sell them, not as fast as they can build them.'

Office of Fair Trading, 2008

The increasing cost of housing, and the decline of home ownership, have risen rapidly up the political agenda in recent years. House prices rose by 259 per cent between 1997 and 2016, while average earnings increased by just 68 per cent. The average home was 7.6 times average earnings in 2016, up from 3.6 times average earnings in 1997.[1] Meanwhile, home ownership has fallen from a high-water mark of 70.9 per cent of households in 2003 to 62.9 per cent in 2015/16, its lowest level since the mid-1980s.[2] Theresa May promised in October 2017 to dedicate her premiership to 'fixing our broken housing market' and building more homes.[3]

In truth, building more homes is only part of the answer to soaring house prices and declining home ownership, which are the result not only of a relatively inelastic supply of new stock but also relaxed mortgage lending, low interest rates, and the attractiveness of housing as an investment. This has encouraged owner-occupiers to bid up prices but it has also attracted into the market additional buyers in the form of domestic buy-to-let landlords and, to a smaller extent, overseas investors. Econometric analysis by Oxford Economics for the Redfern Review into the Decline of Home Ownership found that any shortfalls in supply had made only a marginal difference to house prices since the 1990s, and that enabling output to outstrip household formation would make only a small difference to prices unless sustained over a long period.[4]

But strong housing supply responsive to need is nevertheless essential. It remains the principal tool for reducing the cost of housing *as accommodation,* which is best measured not by the affordability of house prices (which represent the cost of housing *as an investment*) but of rents. The median private rent is equivalent to about a third of household incomes nationally – 27 per cent outside London and 36.6 per cent in London.[5] The UK as a whole has some of the highest housing costs among the advanced economies: the OECD places it seventh highest in a league table of its members on a measure of rents as a proportion of disposable incomes.[6] The cost of housing benefit, which helps low-income households meet unaffordable market rents, has risen in real terms from £3.4 billion in 1980/81 to £25.1 billion in 2015.[7] Meanwhile, homelessness has risen rapidly in recent years, with the number of families in temporary accommodation increasing by more than 50 per cent from 48,010 in 2010 to 78,180 in June 2017; this increase has been driven almost entirely by private tenancies coming to an end and households having nowhere else to go.[8] Expanding the housing stock, especially in those areas where rents are highest proportionate to incomes, is essential to reducing the cost of living in those areas to which people are most drawn. So too is ensuring that the homes that are built are affordable to local people.

It is difficult to be precise about how many new homes are actually needed but the government's official projections were for 236,000 households a year to be formed between 2014 and 2019.[9] However, these projections are lower than the number of new homes that most independent bodies suggest, and indeed what the government acknowledges, is needed. The landmark Barker Review recommended back in 2004 that there would need to be 245,000 private-sector homes a year, plus another 17,000 social housing units.[10] These figures have never been met and Kate Barker, who chaired that review, recently suggested the figure might now need revising up to 300,000 homes a year.[11] The cross-party House of Lords Economic Affairs Committee endorsed this 300,000 figure in July 2016.[12] In the 2017 housing white paper, the government acknowledged a need for between 225,000 and 275,000 homes a year 'to keep up with population growth and start to tackle years of under-supply'.[13]

Housebuilding, meanwhile, has been rising since the financial crisis but the net supply of new homes still only reached 189,650 in 2015/16.[14] There is, then, a disconnect between what is being built and what a widespread consensus of opinion holds to be required. This national picture disguises wide local and regional variations and particularly severe shortfalls in those areas where – unsurprisingly – housing costs are already high. London is the most obvious example, where household growth is expected to average 55,594 per annum for the next 25 years and yet net housing supply was just 30,390 in 2015/16. Most of the fastest-growing local authority areas, including almost all major cities, are failing to build enough homes to keep pace with projected household growth.[15]

Obstacles to higher housing supply

The question is, why aren't we – and why haven't we been – building more homes? It is often noted that there has been a decline in overall output since the 1970s which has corresponded very closely with the decline of local-authority housebuilding. Housing associations, the government's preferred vehicle for affordable housing provision, have increased output but by not nearly enough to have made up the difference. Total output has fallen from in excess of 300,000 a year in the 1960s to little more than half of that in recent years.

The decline of public-sector building is an important part of the story, but not necessarily – as is often implied – because of that fall in total output. In fact, the *net* annual increase in new homes (which is what really counts as a measure of supply) has not changed all that much when the large numbers of demolitions during the post-war decades are also taken into consideration.[16] The important shift in housebuilding since the 1970s does not lie in the decline in gross output so much as the overwhelming reliance on a market-led private-sector model. With the decline of public subsidies for non-market housing, the proportion of output coming from private developers has increased from 50-60 per cent in the 1960s and 1970s to above 80 per cent during most of the 1980s, 1990s and 2000s (Figure 1.1). This means that housing development during this period has mainly been driven by the economic demand for new homes (that is, the availability of buyers willing and able to purchase a new-build) rather than an approximation, however imperfect it might be, of the actual need for housing at any one point in time.

Why does this matter? Basic economic theory would suggest that, with prices rising so quickly, developers

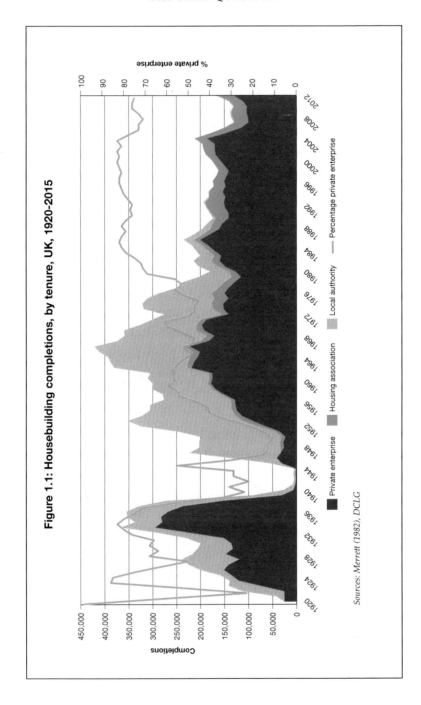

Figure 1.1: Housebuilding completions, by tenure, UK, 1920-2015

Sources: Merrett (1982), DCLG

would respond to the market signal that housing is under-supplied, build more homes and so bring prices back down. But this has not happened. Part of the reason for this lies in the planning system, which is often accused of being overly restrictive. In some places this is true: Savills has calculated that there is a shortfall of 90,000 planning consents a year in those areas of the country where demand is highest.[17] Econometric analysis by Hilber and Vermeulen (2016) suggests regulatory constraints on housebuilding were responsible for a 100 per cent real terms increase in house prices between 1974 and 2008 (out of a total rise of 186 per cent). Green belt restrictions are an essential consideration here. Imposed in the mid-twentieth century to prevent the urban sprawl that had seen the footprint of towns and cities increase rapidly during the 1930s, green belts essentially set the limits to the expansion of many of our urban areas, including London.

But simply approving more land for housing is unlikely on its own to solve many of the difficulties we now face. This has already become apparent in recent years as a substantial increase in planning consents has not resulted in a comparable increase in housebuilding. The discrepancy between the number of homes approved and the number of homes built has become particularly pronounced since the introduction of the National Planning Policy Framework, which was designed to free up the planning system and bring forward more land for development, in 2012.[18] Research by Shelter has found that the number of completed homes between 2011/12 and 2015/16 was just 68 per cent of the number of permissioned units between 2010/11 and 2014/15 (allowing for a one-year lag between approval and construction) – leaving a shortfall of 324,000 homes.[19]

So, while various geographical localities undoubtedly

fail to approve sufficient numbers of homes, this is only one factor holding back development. The focus on planning tends to ignore other important factors that constrain housebuilding and would remain even in the absence of the planning system. These revolve around the private-sector model on which we have become so reliant and, especially, the treatment of land.

Private development and the land market

The fundamental prerequisite for any new housing development is land. For a developer to build new homes, there is nothing they can do without first having the land on which to build them. To secure land that is suitable for new housing the developer must submit a winning bid for it, in competition with other developers with the same intention. This process will establish a market price at which – if it is sufficient incentive for a landowner to part with their site – one developer will be able to take it over and build homes at, hopefully, a profit.

In bidding for the land and thereby establishing the market price, developers must of course work out how much it is worth to them. To do this they will calculate how many homes and of what type they will be able to build on the site; this will be influenced not only by the size of the site but also any planning obligations, such as the provision of sub-market affordable housing and associated infrastructure. They will consider how much it will cost to build those homes, given the price of labour and materials. Finally, they will consider how much they expect to be able to sell those homes for, and so how much revenue the site will generate for them. This will be determined by the current market price for similar homes in the area, possibly with an additional premium given that they are new-build. A crude representation of the valuation would look something like this:

(number of homes x purchase price) *minus* construction costs
minus developer's profit

=

land value

This is the residual land value methodology which dictates that the price paid for the land is effectively all of the profit to be made from the development bar the margin that the developer must be able to secure (usually around 20 per cent) to justify the employment of their capital on the scheme on behalf of shareholders.

The effect of the residual land value model is to ensure that the purchase price of the homes to be built will necessarily be at the top of the potential range. If the site is suitable for three-bedroomed detached houses and three-bedroomed detached houses in the area are currently changing hands for £300,000, it will be impossible for a developer to secure the land with a bid predicated on those homes being sold at, say, £250,000; the developer that worked on the basis of a lower sale price would simply be outbid for the land by a rival with a more aggressive (or realistic) offer.

This model is vitally important for understanding the nature and pace of private housing supply because it means that once the developer gets on site and starts building, they can only do so as quickly as there are buyers coming forward with, in our example, £300,000 for a three-bedroomed house in the given area. Housing supply is in this way determined – and constrained – by what is called the market absorption rate for whatever homes the developer is building. The absorption rate will rarely, if ever, be as fast as the speed at which those homes could technically be built. The Office of Fair Trade described this in 2008:

> ...the homebuilder will build at a rate which will satisfy the demand in the local market at or above the existing price levels... inevitably a homebuilder attempting to offer cheaper homes will be outbid for land by a homebuilder selling homes at the prevailing market price. It is for this reason that build out rates, or absorption rates as they are known... are dictated by local market conditions and not by the maximum technical speed at which homes can be built. Homebuilders deliver new homes as fast as they can sell them, not as fast as they can build them.[20]

This leads to notoriously slow build rates on sites of any size. According to a 2016 study, sites of between 100 and 499 units would deliver on average 60 units a year; a site of 2,000 units or above would still only deliver about 160 a year. Brownfield sites are built considerably more slowly on average than greenfield, however, with those of 500-999 homes being built at a rate of 52 per year, sites of 1,000-1,499 at 73 a year and sites of 1,500-1,999 at 84 a year. These figures suggest a 1,500-unit brownfield site would take more than 17 years to completion even from the point at which work has begun.[21]

Not only is the supply of new homes slower than it could be but it is deliberately so: to build any faster would undermine existing house prices, and therefore the value of the land that the developer has already invested in. The biggest housebuilders are candid about the fact that, having purchased a site, they are not then in a position to build new homes at prices that would undermine existing market prices. As David Thomas, group chief executive of Barratt Developments, told MPs in 2016:

We are clearly not incentivised to sell at below market price. That is not the basis on which we bought the land. If we bought the land on the basis of a below-market-price sale, that would be a different thing.[22]

Peter Redfern, chief executive of Taylor Wimpey, added:

Clearly, we are not looking to drive down the market price, having bought a piece of land, but we are price-takers, not price-setters. We are not looking to control the price and we never have been, either locally or nationally. There is no attempt from the industry to restrict supply, but we are absorbing what demand we can find in the local areas where we have sites, at more or less the market price. That is because that is the financial case on which we have bought the land in the first place.

The price of new-build homes, then, is based on the price that has been paid for the land; the price of the land is based on current market prices; and so new housing supply is limited by the demand for new-build homes at current prices. Developers are acting rationally within this framework and are exposing themselves to considerable risk. Of course, the developer may collect higher profits than anticipated if prices rise above those on which they based their bid for the land: Archer and Cole (2016) show how the nine biggest private housebuilders increased their profit per home built considerably between 2012 and 2015 as the market picked up again following the crash.[23] It must be acknowledged too, however, that developers might find themselves high and dry if house prices fall.

But the biggest winner in this process is not the developer – who is generally seeking a certain margin whether the land price is high or low – but the landowner. Every time a new housing development takes place, the residential value of that site (minus construction costs and the developer's profit margin) is trickling down to the individual or firm who owned the land in its original state. It is the landowner, collecting the residual value of the scheme, who profits most from a drawn-out building process. That the homes are drip-fed into the market over many years keeps property prices high, keeps land prices high and so maximises the landowner's return.

Land ownership and the power of constraint

The system only works like this because the landowner is able to hold out for the maximum price that the current market can bear. Indeed, one of the reasons why the increase in planning permissions has not resulted in a comparable rise in completions is that a lot of land that is approved for development is not even in the hands of a housebuilder. Research suggests that, outside London, more than half of units with outline planning permission but not yet built had been obtained by landowners who are not builders. There is a similar story in London, where 32 per cent of unbuilt planning permissions were held by non-builders in 2014.[24] Before such sites can be developed the owner must agree to sell to a developer.

For some landowners, development might not even have been the reason for seeking planning permission. Some permissions are only sought to increase the value of the land, in order to use it as security for a loan for example, or as a first step towards development before the proposals are fleshed out and the value increased further.[25] Others might simply be waiting for a better offer, in anticipation of a further rise in property values. There is a belief that something like 30-40 per cent of planning permissions do not result in a start, either being reworked and a new permission sought, or never developed at all. Lichfields (2017) points to various reasons for these lapsed permissions, including that they have been sought for 'reasons other than to build out the site', that the landowner 'cannot get the price for the site that will justify the disposal of the asset', that the development 'is not considered financially worthwhile' or a change in priorities of the landowner or developer.

There is a substantial academic literature exploring why landowners frequently choose to wait before making a sale, even if a site is suitable for development at the current time. This work undermines, as McAllister et al (2013) put it, 'the standard neo-classical assumptions that land supply responds to market signals to produce development at the right time, in the right place and at the right price'.[26] It therefore counters the idea that simply approving more land for development will result in proportionately higher levels of output.

To understand why this is, we need to consider that the owner of land with valuable development potential must make an active choice between two courses of action:

1. To develop (or sell for development) immediately, in full knowledge of the market conditions that will apply; or

2. Wait until a future date, by when circumstances and market conditions might have changed, even though there might be uncertainty as to how.

Landowners therefore do not simply choose between rival bidders for their land at a single point in time, today; their choice is between striking the best deal that is available today or waiting to see whether there might be a better deal on offer at a later date. Grovenstein, Kau and Munneke (2011) stress that, if the option to develop has no expiry date, this is an active choice that the owner must take:

This development of vacant land represents a real option held by a landowner and is exercised at the landowner's discretion. The landowner has the ability to postpone development until future market information becomes available.[27]

The weight of such decisions is intensified by the fact that very large amounts of money are at stake and there is only one chance to get the decision right. Guo (2010) sums up the position like this:

> Land development is a typical one-shot decision for private investors due to the huge investment expense and the fear of substantial loss.[28]

Add to this the expectation (often, if not always, correct) that land prices and demand are going to increase in the future, and it is not difficult to see why landowners might rationally hold off a sale indefinitely. Titman (1985) models how the underutilisation of valuable land can result from the rational decision of an owner to postpone building until a future date, when additional information is available, before committing to the precise specifications of a project:

> The fact that investors choose to keep valuable land vacant or underutilized for prolonged periods of time suggests that the land is more valuable as a potential site for development in the future than it is as an actual site for constructing any particular building at the present time.

Titman's modelling suggests that when there is a lot of uncertainty about future property prices, the decision to develop the land at the current time becomes less attractive. If there is little uncertainty, by contrast, then there is less attraction in waiting. He points out that, by this logic, a decision to stimulate demand by reducing interest rates may counter-intuitively lead to a *decrease* in building activity as there is uncertainty in the mind of the landowner about the future of property prices.[29] That is to say, a landowner hopeful that the price may continue to rise may therefore hold off a sale– something that they are less inclined to do if prices have been flat for a period of time.

In a study of land use in Chicago, Grovenstein et al (2011) found evidence of a 'delay premium' which provided developers of office space and high density residential 'incentives to delay investment'. This research followed Quigg (1993) who found that land was traded at values above its intrinsic value which reflected the option to wait to develop. Looking at Seattle, Quigg found a six per cent premium attached to the option to delay.[30] The level of premium the landowner is aspiring to may not even be realistic, however. Adams (2015) traces the presence of so much long-term unused brownfield land (an estimated 17,000 hectares had been derelict in England in 2014) to 'unrealistic owner expectations of what the land is worth':

> Since keeping land vacant incurs no taxation and relatively few holding costs, many landowners are under no pressure to sell, and are quite prepared to wait until that tempting offer finally arrives, even if it never does.[31]

Land for new homes, then, is released at the rate that is in the best economic interests of the landowner. Even if there is competition between a number of landowners in the same area, this does not mean that the price will necessarily fall if they are each prepared to be patient about their sale. This is a key reason why new-build prices are always at the maximum the market will bear, and therefore build rates are slow.

It is useful here to think of the situation not in terms of

houses being built too slowly and in insufficient quantities, but in terms of *residential land being released* too slowly and in insufficient volumes. The asset that is being traded, above all, is not the house that somebody can live in but the land on which it must be built. It is not really the housing component – the bricks and mortar, and the labour that goes into construction – that the market is slow to absorb, it is the land for which the original owner was paid a price that the developer must then recoup from future customers in order to turn a profit.

As a case in point it is worth considering what happened when the housing market turned down after the great financial crisis of 2007/8. UK house prices fell, meaning there were fewer buyers of new-build homes at prices set before the downturn, and so housebuilding slumped. New-build completions fell from 200,300 in 2007/8 to 117,700 in 2010/11.[32] By summer 2012 there were 1,331 stalled building sites, containing 71,821 potential housing units (these all had detailed planning permission but were not being implemented). McAllister et al (2013) found that, while there was a range of factors that influenced whether a site was proceeding or not at this time, nevertheless changed market conditions were 'the key reason for sites becoming stalled'. Depressed prices not only led to lower new-build sales rates, they also increased risk aversion among developers deciding whether to start on a site. In addition to that, landowners were discouraged from selling sites at their new, lower values:

> When the developer/landowner is faced with the changed market circumstances, they have to decide whether to proceed or to, as one interviewee put it he was 'waiting for the market to improve'. This can be equally true for the developer (unwilling to risk the expenditure on getting the

scheme started) and the landowner (not willing to reduce the price they expect to receive for their land). ... Overall, it was clear that the shift in market conditions had created a range of reactions amongst landowners (usually not house-builders) with the result that consents were unlikely to result in construction activity in the short-term.[33]

While there are undoubtedly other factors that influence this process, the ultimate constraint on the supply of land is imposed by the profit-maximising landowner. It will rarely be in the landowner's interest to release land quickly and in some circumstances it may make sense for them to hold onto it for many years.

London

The effects of the dynamic described above are easily observed in London, where the under-supply of housing is most pronounced and where rents and prices are highest. The number of households in London is expected to grow by 55,594 between 2014 and 2039, but net housing supply has not usually been more than half of that in recent years. In 2015/16, it reached 30,390.

These numbers are not, contrary to much contemporary commentary, restricted by the amount of land approved for development. In terms of the simple quantity of homes, enough land has been designated for residential use in recent years to allow the construction of many more homes than have been built. Outline planning permission has been granted for circa 50,000 homes every year for the past decade, according to the Outer London Commission.[34] Some of these planning permissions have not progressed beyond 'outline' stage, meaning that the specifics of the schemes, including Section 106 agreements, have yet to be settled. Developers point to the negotiations of such details

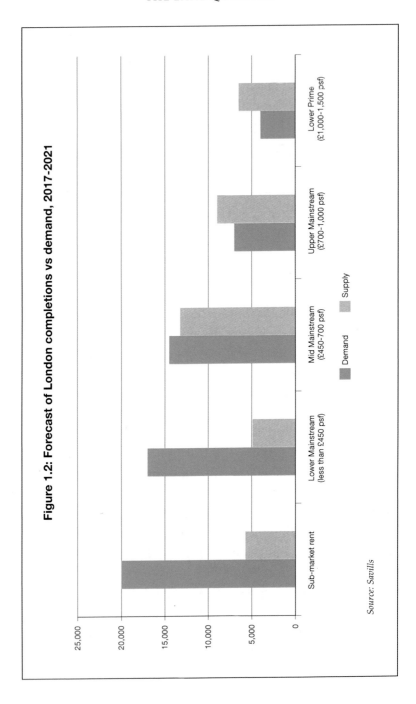

Figure 1.2: Forecast of London completions vs demand, 2017-2021

Source: Savills

and obligations as a substantial barrier to higher output. We will return to the question of Section 106 and the difficulties that presents in Chapter 2. But research by Shelter suggests that even the number of detailed permissions averaged 44,000 a year between 2010/11 and 2014/15.[35] The Mayor of London's draft housing strategy, published in September 2017, points out that the backlog of homes approved but not yet completed had reached a net total of 278,000 in 2015/16. Even if there isn't enough land being approved for development currently, then, there is much more than is being built.

The fundamental weakness of private-sector housing development in London, from a public policy perspective, is that it is catering to a tiny proportion of potential buyers at the highest reaches of the market. This has been picked up in data by Savills, which shows how those homes that are being built are saturating the market for what they term 'upper mainstream' and 'lower prime' housing while failing to provide sufficient homes to meet demand in the lower-priced parts of the market (see Figure 1.2). In the summer of 2017 it found that 58 per cent of housing demand is for homes costing less than £450 per sq. ft., but that this range accounted for only 15 per cent of the building forecast for the next five years. Properties worth more than £1,000 per sq. ft. accounted for only 6.4 per cent of the demand but 21.7 per cent of what was being built.[36]

The practical consequence of this is that the homes that are being built are more difficult for the market to absorb than more affordable output would be, and so the supply of housing is constrained by the availability of buyers to purchase the kind of homes that are being built. This is a natural consequence of landowners holding out for the higher returns that are there to be made in London from the higher end of the market. There is nothing to stop them selling their land at lower prices to target the more affordable end of the market, but there is little incentive for them to do so: even if the market for high-end new-build is saturated now, they always have the option of sitting tight and waiting for the point at which their land is next in line for a higher-end development that will secure them the best return.

London's draft housing strategy acknowledges the 'inherent constraints' on housing supply in a system which relies on private-sector developers to build homes for market sale, including the 'economic limitations on how quickly homes can be sold (whether to would-be occupiers or investors) at the prices required'. About 80 per cent of the new homes build in London are affordable to just eight per cent of households in the capital, a figure that falls further when the upfront costs of house-purchasing are taken into account:

> This means the demand for many new build homes is limited and is strongly correlated with the highly cyclical property market. All of these factors combine to produce build-out rates below levels that would be technically possible without such constraints.[37]

City Hall plans to identify more sites in outer London where land is cheaper, encourage higher density building and support the housing-led redevelopment of many high streets and town centres. But it also stresses that reforms to planning policy alone are 'not enough to ensure that sufficient land will come forward for housing delivery quickly enough, or in a way that always optimises the number of homes developed'. The reasons for this, it says, include:

- Land that could, and should, be developed is often not because land owners lack the incentive to release it, or decide to wait until site values increase to maximise their returns;

- Land that is released, or optioned, is frequently traded rather than developed;

- Developers and home builders, especially in the commercial sector, build at rates which maximise their returns rather than optimising the pace of new supply;

- The speculative nature of development and land trading, coupled with the cyclical nature of the housing market, sets high barriers to entry for new competitors and market 'disrupters', and undermines the ability to secure high levels of affordable homes;

- And councils, who government believes should be proactively addressing these issues and shaping local development, can lack the ability, or inclination, to do so.[38]

Public investment

The inherent limitations of private-sector output are not a new phenomenon. They were well known in the pre-1914 period, when private enterprise was relied upon for virtually all housebuilding. Then, like now, speculative development proceeded in cycles according to the profitable opportunities on offer. It failed over many decades to deal with underlying problems of overcrowding and slum conditions that affected millions of working people. The London County Council, for instance, described a situation in which the construction of working-class homes was limited only to the better-off artisan class of labourer:

> …there is one serious danger in relying wholly upon private enterprise. The provision of the better rented accommodation

suitable for the artisan with a regular income, is a more profitable enterprise than building for the poorer section of the working class... there is not much provision made for families which can only afford to pay for two or three rooms.[39]

By the outbreak of the First World War, a consensus had begun to emerge about the need for public subsidies for the provision of housing that was uneconomical for the private sector to build. Overcrowding had improved slightly during the 1890s, down from 33 per cent to 28.6 per cent, but made no further progress over the following decade. Between 1901 and 1911, while London's population rose by 670,000, enough to occupy 580,000 rooms, its net stock rose by only 400,000 rooms. Meanwhile, rents – which had risen during the 1890s – merely plateaued at their new level in the first decade of the twentieth century.[40] The speculative building industry had no answers to this 'acknowledged evil', as *The Times* described it in a leading article in 1913:

It is admitted on all sides that the housing of the working classes both in town and country districts urgently needs improvement, and that the homes of a large proportion of the nation fall far beneath the standard of health, decency, and comfort which our level of civilization requires... Private enterprise is proved to be incapable of solving the problem by itself, where it has hitherto been left to deal with it.[41]

On the eve of the First World War, the chancellor David Lloyd George told the Commons: 'You cannot provide houses in this country by private enterprise.'[42] For much of the twentieth century, these problems were largely overcome by major public-sector housebuilding programmes which effectively topped up for-sale housebuilding to achieve centrally-agreed national targets based on estimates of need. Between 1921 and 1939, local authority housebuilding rose from negligible levels in the pre-war era to an average output of about 70,000 a year, with peaks of 121,000 in both 1929 and 1939.[43] Between 1948 and 1972, local authority completions never dropped below 100,000 per annum and in 1953 and 1954 they even rose above 200,000. By the 1970s, ministers were able to point to a crude surplus in housing.[44] Success during both of these periods was owed to the combined efforts of the public and private sectors.

Since the late 1960s, however, council housebuilding has been scaled back, as subsidies were reduced, borrowing caps were imposed on local authority housing revenue accounts and Right to Buy forced the sale of stock without the proceeds being made available for new construction. In recent years housebuilding output by English councils has settled at between about 1,000 and 2,000 a year. Since the 1980s, public subsidies for housebuilding have been mostly channelled through housing associations, but their output has been a fraction of the former local authority output.

Since 2010, capital grants for non-market housing have been reduced still further, leading to a halving in the number of grant-funded affordable homes, from 55,909 in 2010/11 to 27,792 in 2016/17. This has resulted in the long-term decline of council and housing association accommodation (from 5.5 million units in 1981 to 4 million units in 2016). Moreover, because of changes to the definition of 'affordable'- which now includes homes of up to 80 per cent of market rents – most of those homes are in fact much less affordable than they would have been previously. Construction for traditional social rent, which is pegged to local incomes and usually around 40-50 per cent of market rents, has fallen from 36,713 to 1,102 over the same period.[45]

Concurrent to this, there has been a steep rise in the number of people in private rented housing.[46] The housing benefit bill – paid to support low-income households who cannot afford market rents – has risen from £3.4 billion in 1980/81 to £25.1 billion in 2015/16 (in real terms).[47] Of that, £9.1m was paid last year into the private rented sector: a direct state transfer to landlords towards rents that would otherwise be unaffordable. Analysis by the City consultancy Capital Economics projects that housing benefit spending will increase to almost £62 billion (in today's prices) in 2065/67, of which the private sector will account for £38 billion.[48]

Conclusion

While there is a case for ensuring that the planning system is more responsive to need, housing supply is unlikely to reach levels that would bear down significantly on prices: builders are, as they say, price-takers not price-makers. It is difficult to see how the present housing difficulties can be overcome without renewed public investment in the types of homes we need. This could be achieved by the return of local-authority building at scale. With the Conservative Party now supporting a new generation of council housing, the three main parties in England agree on the need for a local-authority building programme.

As of late 2017, however, the government's ambitions remained limited to council building in the low thousands per annum, funded out of central government's affordable housing budget. But if this is to be scaled up to meaningful numbers, it will require a substantial increase in levels of spending. There is a clear way forward for achieving this, for which town halls have been lobbying for many years: remove the caps on their housing revenue accounts so that they are free to borrow to invest in new homes, and restore to them all future receipts from Right to Buy, ensuring the sale of council homes funds the construction of more of them.

There is a danger in such a scenario, however, that the dynamics of the land market described above would come into play. By increasing the demand for residential land in the places that need homes most, it would drive up the cost of that land not only for local authorities but for private builders too. For both private and public-sector homes to be built more quickly, residential land needs to be released more quickly and at lower prices. The obstacle to that is the landowner's ability in most circumstances to sit out a fall in prices and wait for values to rise again, potentially for long periods of time. As well as a renaissance in council building, we need to reform the land market in such a way that landowners are incentivised to part with sites for new housing development sooner rather later, even if that means settling for much lower prices than have become customary.

2

Land values and where they go

'The reputable builder does not normally look for his profits to the sale of land.'

Lewis Silkin, 1947

'Despite appearances, housebuilding is only partially the business of putting up houses. The houses are the socially acceptable side of making profits out of land appreciation.'

Investor's Chronicle, 1974

The framework described in the previous chapter delivers vast windfalls for the owners of that land suitable for new housing. The scale of this is revealed by the average valuations for agriculural, industrial and residential land respectively; when land is developed for new housing it has usually undergone a change of use, sanctioned via the planning system, from agricultural or industrial to residential. A hectare of land in England had an average agricultural use value of £21,000 in 2015, varying very little by region. With planning permission for residential development, however, a hectare outside London was worth on average £2.1 million – 100 times as much. In London, the value of a hectare of residential land was many times higher still: in Redbridge, an outer borough, it would have cost about £9.2 million; in Kensington and Chelsea, in the centre of the capital, it would have been £134 million a hectare (see Figure 2.1).[1]

Landowners raised an estimated £12.4 billion in profits from land sold for housing in 2014/15, according to the Centre for Progressive Capitalism.[2] A small amount of this, £322 million, constituted public sector land sales, and another £2.8 billion was recouped by local authorities from 'developer contributions' (via Section 106 agreements and the Community Infrastructure Levy, discussed further below). But that left an estimated profit for private landowners of £9.3 billion. This means that for each new home built that year, £60,000 on average went to the original landowner (or was shared between various landowners who may have traded it over a period of time prior to development).

Such profits enjoyed by a relatively tiny number of people – there are usually roughly 15-20,000 projects approved each year – are the flipside of the housing affordability crisis we are grappling with today: the more house prices rise, the more landowners can command for sites suitable for new housing. And, as we saw in the previous chapter, these sums are achieved only by the drawn-out release of new residential land, of which slow build rates are a part, and of construction focusing on the more expensive sections of the market.

The price differential between agricultural land and residential land has always been pronounced, at least since the advance of urbanisation in the late 18th and early 19th centuries, resulting in large windfall gains for those whose land is gradually absorbed by the nearest town or city. But today's residential land values are of a different magnitude to earlier periods, due to the rapid real-terms increase in house prices over recent decades and particularly since the mid-1990s. Development land values being a function of

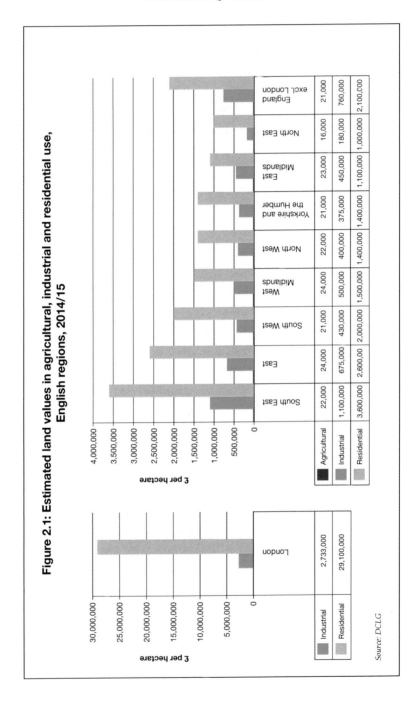

Figure 2.1: Estimated land values in agricultural, industrial and residential use, English regions, 2014/15

	South East	East	South West	West Midlands	North West	Yorkshire and the Humber	East Midlands	North East	England excl. London
Agricultural	22,000	24,000	21,000	24,000	22,000	21,000	23,000	16,000	21,000
Industrial	1,100,000	675,000	430,000	500,000	400,000	375,000	450,000	180,000	760,000
Residential	3,600,000	2,600,000	2,000,000	1,500,000	1,400,000	1,400,000	1,100,000	1,000,000	2,100,000

	London
Industrial	2,733,000
Residential	29,100,000

£ per hectare

Source: DCLG

36

the price that a new-build home can fetch, they have risen correspondingly since the beginning of the 1970s, when house prices began to accelerate (see Figure 2.2).

There are various factors that have generated that house price growth and more than a little disagreement about what has been the most important. Developers and free-marketeers tend to point to the restrictions introduced on housebuilding by post-war land-use planning and the introduction of the green belt that effectively fixed the outer limits of many of our towns and cities in the 1950s. This, as referenced already in Chapter 1, is supported by econometric modelling by Hilber and Vermeulen that suggests real house prices in England would have risen about 100 per cent less between 1974 and 2008 if 'all regulatory constraints were removed'; that is, house prices would have been about 35 per cent lower, rising from £79,000 in 1974 to £147,000 instead of to £226,000 in 2008.[3] Their analysis implies that, without any planning controls at all, real house prices would still have risen by 86 per cent during the same period. Others have pointed to the influence of relaxed credit conditions since the early 1970s and the impact of low interest rates since the 1990s in particular. This has facilitated an historically-unprecedented expansion of mortgage lending since the 1970s (see Figure 2.3).

Muellbauer (2012) describes credit supply conditions as the 'elephant in the room', pointing out that similar house price growth has taken place in countries that have embraced similarly liberal credit markets since the 1970s.[4] Oxford Economics (2016) plays down the significance of supply constraints in the house price boom that has taken place since the mid-1990s. Its modelling suggests that most of the real-terms increase in house prices in the decade after 1996 came from earnings growth (107 percentage

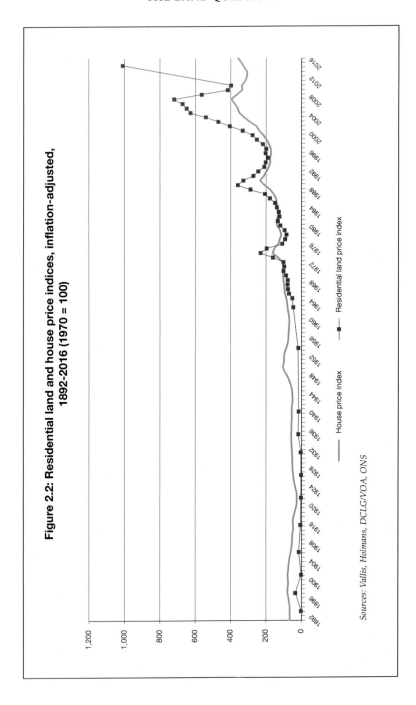

Figure 2.2: Residential land and house price indices, inflation-adjusted, 1892-2016 (1970 = 100)

Sources: Vallis, Holmans, DCLG/VOA, ONS

points of the 151 per cent rise). The next most significant determinant (accounting for 38 percentage points) was the fall in mortgage interest rates, which reduced the user cost of capital for investors. Oxford Economics calculates that building an additional 100,000 units to housing supply in excess of household formation in any given year would reduce prices by just 0.6 per cent.[5]

Irrespective of precisely where we place the greatest emphasis, there can be little dispute that house price growth is the outcome of a large increase in purchasing power on a quantity of housing stock that is relatively inelastic. Singling out the planning system here, however, tends to overlook the fact that the supply of land in locationally desirable areas is inelastic by its very nature and was subject to speculation long before the planning system was introduced (see Chapter 3). Moreover, while there is little doubt that planning has amplified housing and land prices, it was introduced in the first place to tackle the failings of the laissez-faire housebuilding that pre-dated it, by giving local authorities more control over what was built and where, and ensuring that land could not be withheld from use for the public good in the pursuit of private profit by the individual landowner. An essential element of this was a land-values policy – since abolished – that discouraged speculation on land and held down prices.

Land-values policy 1947-1959

The planning system as we know it today is largely the product of the 1947 Town and Country Planning Act, which for the first time brought almost all development under control by making it subject to planning permission. Town planning had been evolving through a series of pieces of legislation since 1909 but until this point it was patchily

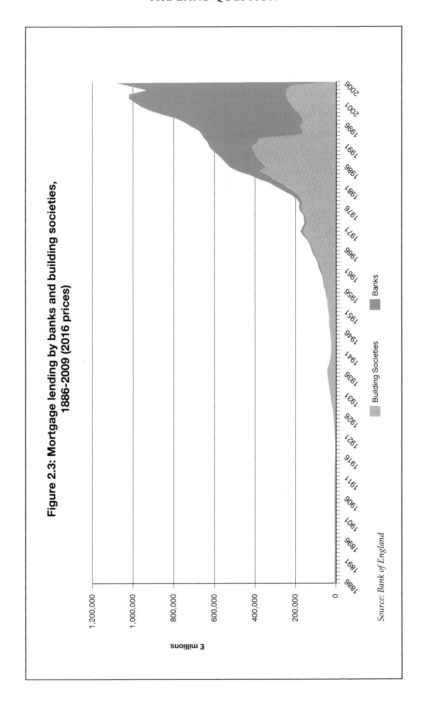

Figure 2.3: Mortgage lending by banks and building societies, 1886-2009 (2016 prices)

£ millions

Banks

Building Societies

Source: Bank of England

adopted by local authorities and mostly unenforced.[6] From 1947, planning permission became a pre-requisite for development and it is the granting of that permission today (and/or the anticipation of it) that secures for the landowner the windfalls described previously. But the appropriation of this increase in value, or 'betterment' as it has often been known, by the owner was never the intention of the authors of the 1947 Act. This legislation followed many years of inquiries and debate in Whitehall about land-use planning, which included lengthy consideration of the impact it would have in generating large profits for some landowners – by squeezing development values into a smaller number of potential sites – while denying it to others who were refused the right to develop. This had been the focus of the Uthwatt Committee in particular, which was commissioned in 1941 to consider:

> … (a) possible means of stabilising the value of land required for development or redevelopment and (b) any extension or modification of powers to enable such and to be acquired by the public on an equitable basis…

Holding down land prices and acquiring it at 'equitable' prices was of paramount importance to the architects of the 1947 planning system due to the difficulties local authorities had experienced during the inter-war period in exercising their supposed planning prerogatives. A compensation regime requiring councils to reimburse landowners for any loss of value that resulted from the use of planning powers rendered them mostly inoperable.[7] A wide range of potential responses to this were considered by Uthwatt and ministers of the day, including full land nationalisation, to which the Labour Party was committed under its 1918 constitution.

The approach eventually adopted in the 1947 Act was

instead to tax all of the increase in value arising from planning permission, by way of a development charge set at 100 per cent of the difference between existing use value and residential use value. This meant that there would be no profit to be made for landowners from change of use – all of the additional value would accrue to the state. On the compensation side, for landowners *denied* planning permission, payment was only to be made in recognition of land 'dead ripe' for development in 1947; future claims against the state for loss of value would not be permitted.

The intention was for builders to purchase land for new homes at their existing use value and then pay the development charge (equivalent to the increase in the value of the land) to the newly-created Central Land Board. Their profit would be made on their housebuilding alone, not on land trading. As the planning minister Lewis Silkin told MPs when the bill was introduced for its Second Reading in the House of Commons:

> The reputable builder does not normally look for his profits to the sale of land. He expects to make a profit out of his building operations, and this he will be able to do when the Bill becomes law just as much as he could before. In so far as he does look to making his profits out of the sale of land, this is a practice which I regard as undesirable, and no harm will come to the community if it is no longer possible.[8]

The development charge did not last long, however. It was deeply unpopular among landowners, became difficult to enforce and was scrapped by the subsequent Conservative government under the 1953 Town and Country Planning Act.

The failure of the development charge is instructive and lay in the inevitable resistance to it from landowners, who faced binding restrictions on how they could use their land

and could no longer profit even when their schemes were approved. Their opposition had major practical implications, because a 100 per cent tax left no profit incentive for them to part with their land for development. The response from many was to refuse to sell, hindering the supply of land for new homes. To overcome this, the Central Land Board was meant to be able to compulsorily-purchase land, but its powers were badly drafted – the legislation referring to racketeering rather than hoarding – and they were not properly used. There was also resistance to compulsory purchase being used in this way from the Treasury, where officials felt such matters should be left to the market. As Cox (1984) writes, however:

> This was a misconception because it failed to take into account that land withholding by recalcitrant owners (who saw no profit in selling land at existing use value) would be the major difficulty rather than racketeering in land prices. Officials in the Ministry of Town and Country Planning had always envisaged that, in the interim period of the Act's life, the Central Land Board would have to use its planning powers extensively to overcome the owners' ability to act negatively to frustrate the Act's intentions. The wording of the 1947 Act, however, left the Board's compulsory purchase role ambiguous and this led to its failure. ... The real difficulty was that the 100 per cent charge was imposed on a market which was free to act in its own way.[9]

It is worth noting that the extent to which land hoarding really impacted on housebuilding output during this period is not clear-cut. Private-enterprise building was anyway limited by the 1945-51 Labour government to no more than a fifth of new homes (the rest being reserved for local-authority homes). Cullingworth and Nadin (2006) suggest that 'within the limits of the building activity set by the Labour government (1945-51), it is unlikely that the development charge procedure seriously affected the supply of land [but] it is probable that the [1951] Conservative government's plans for private building would have been jeopardised by it'.[10]

Public-sector purchases 1947-1959

The development charge on private-sector building was only one part of this land-values policy, however. As part of the same regime, local authorities were also able to aquire land for their own development purposes at existing use value. And when the development charge was abolished in 1953 the situation for councils hardly changed: they were allowed to continue purchasing land, compulsorily if necessary, at existing use value plus any development value at 1947 values.[11] This meant that, after 1953 and the abolition of the development charge on private land sales, there was left a dual land market. Land purchased compulsorily by the state was valued at existing use and that purchased privately at its full market rate – including the development value that planning permission conferred. This situation intensified the sense of grievance among those landowners forced to sell to the state who, writes Connellan (2004), 'considered themselves to be very badly treated in comparison with those who were able to sell their land at increased prices, resulting partially from the planning restrictions on other sites'.[12] A headline in *The Times* on August 8, 1958, read: 'LAND OWNERS GET A RAW DEAL'.[13] The following year the policy was overturned and the return to a free market in land was completed. Under the 1959 Town and Country Planning Act local authorities were required to purchase land at its full residential value once more.

But for 11 years, between 1948 (when the 1947 Act was

implemented) and 1959, councils were able to buy land for their housebuilding programmes at, or close to, existing use value. About 1.8m local authority homes were built in England during this period, more than a third of the 4.5m that have been built since the Second World War.[14] It is unclear how much resort local authorities had to compulsory purchase – the very existence of this power held land prices down and may have encouraged landowners to strike deals with councils. As the then housing minister Harold Macmillan told the House of Commons in 1953:

> If the land owner or his representatives do not ask more than moderate prices, it may not be necessary to have recourse to this weapon, but the fact that this power exists and will be exercised is an immense weapon to prevent exploitation.[15]

Across roughly the same period, the new town development corporations also had powers to acquire land at existing use value. The new towns programme, conducted in three main phases between 1946 and 1970, took as its inspiration the two garden cities of the earlier twentieth century. Letchworth, begun in 1903, and Welwyn Garden City, begun in 1919, were both built on land that had been purchased at agricultural use value, the residential purpose of the purchases simply being kept secret from local landowners at that time.[16] The post-war development corporations, set up under the New Towns Act 1946, were given formal powers to compulsorily purchase the land required – and at current-use value – if it could not be bought by voluntary agreement. While the corporations had the power to compulsorily-purchase land in this way, in fact the threat of this was usually sufficient for the land to be assembled mostly by agreement. This rendered those developments highly profitable for the development corporations, whether property was rented (as it usually was in the earlier stages) or sold at market values:

> This made it possible to reduce the land costs in delivery of housing (or other buildings, including public and community facilities) to extraordinarily low levels. At comparable early stages in their development, the unserviced land cost component of houses in Harlow and Milton Keynes has been demonstrated to have been only about one per cent of housing costs at the time. Obviously this had major long term implications for the profitability of the New Towns, since renting or disposal of assets could reap handsome profits.[17]

Twenty-one new towns were developed in England (32 in the UK) under this land-purchase framework in the post-war period, and they provide homes for about 2.8m people today.[18]

The land-values policy under which the new towns were developed was undone by the 1961 Land Compensation Act, which determined that landowners were in future to be paid the value of the land including any hope value. This incorporated the no-scheme world, or Pointe Gourde, principle that landowners were not to receive compensation for any additional value that was brought about by the scheme giving rise to the compulsory purchase. However, that did not exclude the possibility that land would have been used for residential purposes even in the absence of the scheme in question, and so land acquisition became prohibitively costly in the years ahead.

Land speculation since 1959

The land-values policy introduced after the Second World War facilitated cheap public investment in housing but it also, as it was intended to, served to hold land values down under the new planning regime. That is not to say some land for new housing did not change hands at above its existing use value: the post-war rationing of building licences meant that possession of the right to build was often incentive enough for a developer to pay more than that, even if the development charge meant they would have to pay twice. Nevertheless, it was not until the 1960s, after the land-values policy was dismantled, that prices escalated. Cox (1984) writes:

> As long as owners could expect to receive only existing use value there was little point in buying land to hold in anticipation of a price rise. But when development values were given back to private sellers the prospect of speculative profits emerged again.[19]

This began in part even after the half-way abolition of the existing-use value regime in 1953. From the mid-1950s there was an increase in demand for land from growing numbers of firms and individuals seeking to move into property development, including entrepreneurs, financial institutions, supermarket chains and department stores. But until 1959 there remained the possibility that land could be compulsorily-purchased by the state at its existing use value. After the return to a free market in land under the 1959 Act (with some exemptions for new towns and for local authorities undertaking redevelopment and expansion) prices began to escalate much more quickly. Merrett (1979) points to a 'price watershed' dating from that year.[20] Cox (1984) suggests that the demand for residential land exceeded the underlying demand for housing:

> This increase was probably only partially related to the rise in the level of demand for houses from consumers and may have been largely determined by each individual builder assuming that he would be able to maximise his share of the market. In other words, each builder, seeing a

potential consumer demand, would assume he could sell every house he could build. Thus, the number of firms in the market seeking profits would eventually determine land prices much more than the 'real' demand from consumers. This is not a problem for builders if they are able to pass on increased land prices in the form of rising house prices, and so long as consumer demand is high.[21]

The Macmillan government sought to address this by encouraging local authorities to release more land for development, arguing that too little land rather than speculation was the cause of the increase in values.[22] But land prices only continued to rise in the decades ahead – with a couple of spectacular booms and busts along the way. The price of residential land rose from (in 2016 prices) about £150,000 a hectare in the early 1950s to about £5m a hectare in 2007. Much of this increase occurred from the mid-1990s, when an average hectare of land with outline planning permission for residential development was still only £1.3m.[23]

For local authorities (and, later, housing associations), the rising cost of land has absorbed large chunks of housebuilding budgets. Soon after 1959, land acquisition costs for council housing rose rapidly, doubling in just four years between 1963 and 1967, for example. The land component of the cost of building a council home rose from 7.1 per cent in 1963 to 19 per cent by 1975. Total local authority capital expenditure on housebuilding rose from £5.2 billion in 1963 to £12.5 billion in 1975 (2016 prices).[24] Land acquisition costs for the average local authority home had risen from £3,843 to £17,705 over the same 12-year period.[25] These numbers were still very small compared with today, however: real residential land values rose more than seven-fold between 1975 and 2007.

Later betterment levies

After the failure of the 1947 regime, there were further attempts to impose development taxes – at lower levels – in the following decades, but none survived. One was a betterment levy introduced by Labour under the Land Commission Act of 1967, this time charged at just 40 per cent of the development value (although meant to be increased by stages). This was abolished in 1970. There was then a further Labour attempt to impose a development land tax in 1976, initially to be charged at 80 per cent and with a view to it rising eventually to 100 per cent. However, this was reduced to 60 per cent by the new Conservative government in 1979, and was then abolished altogether in 1985.[26]

There were various difficulties with these initiatives which led to their ultimate demise. One lay in how to assess precisely how much of an increase in land value there had been in any particular case. This required estimations of the value of the land in its existing use value which could be (and was often) contested. This difficulty is inherent in any system of taxing increments in land value separate from the structures upon it.

The other, more intractable problem was that betterment levies disincentivised the sale of land, and especially so if there was any prospect of them being repealed or relaxed by a future administration. The 1947 system was typical in that respect. That regime, however, did not even offer the prospect of short-term reward, because the tax was levied at 100 per cent; there was therefore simply no money to be made by a landowner selling their land for development. This was a fatal flaw in a mechanism which (in the absence of a working compulsory-purchase mechanism) depended on landowners doing just that. It is worth noting that there were various voices that advocated setting the charge at a more moderate level. Silkin had suggested it should be set at 70 or 80 per cent to ensure there was at least something for the landowner.[27] Similarly, before the subsequent Churchill government abolished it, chancellor Rab Butler had suggested merely reducing the development tax to 60 or 70 per cent. Instead it went from one extreme to the other.

But even the later levies, that were charged at lower percentages, disincentivised development and land hoarding ensued. Blundell (1993) writes:

> For owners of developable land, waiting was often no problem. Land, they observed, always increases in value in the long run. They had nothing to lose. Instead of more building land becoming available for development, there was less.[28]

Just as today the owners of land can keep prices high by withholding it until what they judge to be the most opportune moment, attempts to claw back some of that value were stymied by the same tendency. There is little incentive for them to compromise on price in order to secure a sale, which means housing land is brought forward and developed at a slow pace. But it also means that if a tax is introduced on the windfall profits they make as a result of that activity, they can refuse to sell and wait for the tax to be abolished.

Section 106

In the absence of a lasting, formal mechanism for capturing betterment, local authorities from the 1980s increasingly resorted to negotiated private agreements with developers as a condition of planning permission being granted. Initially targeted at the provision of off-site infrastructure, these 'developer contributions' came to be used more and more for securing affordable housing as local authority building dried up.[29] This approach was pursued more systematically from 1990, when the government overtly began shifting to the private sector the cost of providing affordable housing,[30] and the framework for negotiated obligations was consolidated in the Town and Country Planning Act of that year.

Under Section 106 (s106) of that Act, councils have been able to stipulate how much of each development should be made up of affordable, non-market housing. If the developer was unwilling to meet this requirement, councils could in theory refuse permission. Agreements vary considerably on a case-by-case basis but typical would be a requirement for in the region of 20-40 per cent of the new homes to be sub-market provision. The higher the value of the scheme, the more that will generally be required in contributions, with the biggest developments possibly involving the provision of highways works, public transport, education and community facilities, play areas and so on.[31]

The s106 process is a way of securing development profit towards community provision including affordable housing. The cost of selling units (to housing associations, say) at sub-market prices and providing other infrastructure may be borne by the developer but, in theory at least, this cost should be passed on to the landowner in a lower bid for the land. In this way, s106 has become the main tool for capturing increases in land values in recent decades and – to its credit – has bedded in much better than any of the predecessor schemes ever did. Its negotiated nature, however, has long been a source of tension and has in recent years become an increasingly contentious aspect of housing policy.

As far back as 2004, the system was described by the Office of the Deputy Prime Minister as 'opaque, slow, unfair, complex and reactive'.[32] The Barker Review of Housing also identified a series of weaknesses in the s106 regime, including the fact that negotiations can 'take many months, occasionally years, and are costly in both local authority and developer time and resources'; it also pointed to asymmetries in negotiating expertise between developers and local authorities, and a lack of awareness on the part of local authorities of what would constitute a reasonable contribution under s106; on the other hand, some local authorities might misuse s106 to 'delay or discourage development'.[33]

For their part, developers have long resented what can seem to them a development tax by another name. Local authorities, meanwhile, feel that developers hold the whip hand in negotiations given that they have been, since the 1980s, increasingly dependent on the private sector for the vast majority of new housebuilding, affordable or otherwise. This renders it difficult for councils to negotiate the necessary contributions because they feel unable to sacrifice the development altogether.

So as well as creating delays and uncertainty, the s106 often fails to secure the affordable housing that an area requires. This last is partly due to the fact that the nature of the s106 process makes it difficult for the costs of such contributions to be capitalised into land prices at an earlier stage so that the incidence is on the original landowner rather than the developer.[34] Grant (1990) describes:

> ...a lack of certainty and predictability as to the demands likely to be made by a local planning authority which, were they more readily forecastable, could more readily be translated into land price at an earlier stage.[35]

Recent changes to the planning regime have exacerbated these difficulties. When the market downturn that followed the 2007/8 financial crisis rendered many developments unprofitable to proceed with, the Coalition government stepped in to help by encouraging local authorities to revisit s106 agreements and reduce previously-agreed obligations on developers so that stalled sites would become 'viable' once more. Of course this did nothing about the fact that developers had essentially paid more for land than they could ultimately realise through their schemes, and so affordable housing was sacrificed to protect the developers' bottom line.[36]

The concept of 'viability' testing was enshrined in the National Planning Policy Framework (NPPF), introduced in 2012, which stated that there must be a 'competitive' return for both developer and landowner so that the project would be economically viable. This was intended, reasonably, to ensure planning requirements were not a barrier to higher levels of housebuilding. But it has created a circular situation in which, if developers overpay for the land given the s106 obligations tied to it, they can then negotiate those obligations down on 'viability' grounds. Because of the competitive nature of the land market, this is now one more tool available to developers when trying to secure a site.

The Royal Institution of Chartered Surveyors has described the risks inherent in this situation, where a landowner's decision to release new land for development may be influenced by 'any expectation that they can use the existing planning policy framework to reduce the amount of planning obligations that will have to be paid to the community', which may also influence the price a developer may be prepared to pay a landowner:[37]

> ... if there is uncertainty over the level of planning obligations payable then this will increase the option value element of

land value (due to increased volatility), thus increasing land values. This can lead to higher land prices in the market and a threshold land value [the price at which a landowner will be persuaded to sell] that is based on market value will also increase. Developers will appeal to have planning obligations reduced and, if successful, this creates an environment of further uncertainty (as local authorities review their planning obligation targets downwards), higher land prices and the process repeats.[38]

The implication is that developers effectively pay sums for land on the assumption that they can later appeal against the s106 obligations that come with it. There is mounting empirical evidence that this has indeed been the case. But, as we have seen already, it is not the developers who are the real winners when prices are bid up but the landowners who have been paid for land at levels that do not allow for the required s106 obligations. As Sayce et al (2017) find in a study of the situation in London:

> ...the cumulative changes to planning policies since 2012, as operated in practice, have had the effect of shifting the balance of power between developers, landowners and community with the result that landowners have been the primary beneficiaries, to the detriment of the delivery of policy compliant development... This has produced a circular situation in which the more a developer pays for a site, the lower the s106 contributions can be argued.[39]

The circularity is compounded by the fact that transactions which have been 'predicated on the hope, assumption or prediction' that the contribution could be reduced through negotation or on appeal, are then used as a benchmark for viability appraisals related to other schemes.[40] The negotiated nature of s106 obligations always undermined the scope for obligations to be priced into land values, but the viability regime worsened the situation and in the process emboldened landowners prepared to hold out for higher offers. This has had implications for the supply of new land for housing:

> It was acknowledged that in some cases landowners are reluctant to bring land into the market – or at least at prices which truly reflect stated affordable housing policy compliance; and this high or inflated expectation, built on the ability to negotiate contributions downward has been a driver of land prices, with developers acknowledging that they have had to bid in excess of values supportable through residual valuations reflecting s106 policies. So, landowners have been confident in delaying development until such time as they can achieve a price which satisfies their ambitions. If they think that values will increase – they are prepared to wait maybe for the long term.[41]

This has led to the perverse position where declining numbers of affordable housing are secured from developer contributions while the profits on development land have accelerated. In London, a 92.5 per cent increase in house prices and an accompanying 144.8 per cent increase in residential land values has corresponded with a 37 per cent decline in affordable housing delivery.

Separate research (McAllister, Shepherd and Wyatt; forthcoming) has found that the percentage of site value that is captured by developer contributions in inner London has fallen dramatically over the past decade or so, from an estimated 70 per cent in 2005 to about 49 per cent in 2017. This has been the result not only of the viability regime but of the introduction of the 'affordable rent' tenure (as opposed to traditional 'social rent') which is less costly to developers to provide but more expensive for tenants. To have levied the same proportion of land value capture via developer contributions in 2017 as in 2005, non-market housing provision would have needed to be 39 per cent of a development on average, whereas in reality it was in the region of 25 per cent. McAllister et al say:

> Changes in estimated relative land value capture were caused by both changes in market conditions and changes in the policy regime for developer contributions. Broadly, the policy environment for the capture of land value was not updated to keep pace with the rapid increases in residential values relative to non-land development costs so that the application of policy captured a declining proportion of land value over time.[42]

In other words, developer contributions have been falling while land values have been rising, meaning that more of the profit from developments has been flowing to the landowner. This is the result of a regime that has greatly tilted the balance of power in the favour of developers over local authorities, enabling developers to bargain their affordable housing contributions down below levels the local authority feels are appropriate and/or necessary.[43]

Despite these failings, and because of the decline in capital funding, s106 is now the tool local authorities rely on most for the provision of sub-market housing. In a recent survey, 65 per cent of councils said most of their social and affordable housing was delivered via s106.[44] This would not be a reliable source of delivery even were the system to work as intended, as it relies on the strength of the private housebuilding industry, with affordable output cut in line with market output during periodic downturns.[45] Worse than that, however, even when private development is increasing in profitability, s106 provision is prone to being squeezed out.

Community Infrastructure Levy

The difficulties with s106 illustrate the need for greater certainty about the demands that will be placed on development in order to, first, ensure that democratically-agreed planning objectives are adhered to rather than being watered down by landowners and/or developers, and second, so that those demands can be capitalised into land prices at an early stage in the process. This is what the Community Infrastructure Levy (CIL), introduced in 2010, was designed in part to achieve. This enables local authorities to collect developer contributions to off-site infrastructure needs arising from the development. Unlike s106, it is not negotiated but charged according to a fixed schedule on the development of new floorspace. In areas where it is used, s106 agreements are scaled back to be used only for on-site infrastructure and affordable housing provision.

Designed to be fairer, faster and more certain than s106, CIL has had mixed reviews in the years since it was introduced and, in November 2015, the then communities secretary Greg Clark announced a review of its operation to date. This review was published alongside the housing white paper in February 2017 and reported various teething troubles and weaknesses:

- Implementation has been patchy, especially in the north, midlands and Wales. Only 130 authorities have introduced a CIL although another 88 are working towards it, which would provide coverage of just under 60 per cent of charging authorities. Adoption was concentrated in London and the South East, with less affluent areas concerned about 'actual or perceived' viability implications because of lower land prices.

- There are numerous exemptions and reliefs attached to CIL that introduce complexity and reduce its money-raising potential. In some areas, more than 40 per cent of development was exempted.

- It is raising 'materially less' money than was intended. The review estimated that it might raise £4.7 billion to £6.8 billion over a 10-year period, or £470-£680 million a year. Even in those areas where it is used, it is yielding only between five per cent and 20 per cent of the funding required for new infrastructure.

The review team received positive responses regarding CIL from less than 10 per cent of those councils who have either implemented it already or plan to. Many developers also did not like it, and 'seem to have discovered a nostalgic fondness for the s106 process, notwithstanding all their previous complaints about it'.

The problems that have been encountered with CIL illustrate, ironically, the strengths of s106. Where s106 is flexible, the rigidity of CIL presents viability challenges for many sites. This has led to a situation where CIL is set low to accommodate the least viable proposals with the consequence that other projects are paying less than they would have done under s106. The introduction of exemptions and reliefs meanwhile reduces the simplicity which is meant to be CIL's redeeming quality.[46] Setting the CIL charges is a complicated business for local authorities therefore, and can be 'lengthy and expensive', with costs ranging from £15,000 to £50,000 to commission work and manage the process.

This is important not only because infrastructure needs can hold up new housebuilding but because pressure on local services can be a powerful driver of opposition to new homes, or Nimbyism ('Not in my back yard'). A study for the Department for Communities and Local Government, looking at attitudes to housebuilding, found that 'pressure on infrastructure and services was often the main reason for opposition to housing development'. Some 44 per cent of people who would usually oppose development would be less opposed if there was more investment in infrastructure and services (another 15 per cent answered 'maybe').[47]

Conclusion

There has been widespread dissatisfaction with s106 and CIL and the present government is committed to improving the system of developer contributions. In the housing white paper in February 2017, it promised to examine options for wider reform.[48] The outcomes of the current system have worsened in recent years but its difficulties have been longstanding and are inherent to a system of negotiated contributions, which create room for delay and uncertainty and are liable to be gamed by developers and landowners. CIL has, in practice, failed to provide an adequate alternative. It is effectively a return to a betterment levy, a fixed sum but set locally. The teething troubles it has faced in implementation and the small sums that it has raised are a reminder of the reasons why the betterment taxes of the 1940s, 1960s and 1970s failed – taxing development at too high a level will deter land release for development.

The weakness in all of these schemes lies in the attempt to claw back the increase in value after it has been generated by way of a tax on, or an agreement with, the developer. The concept of developer contributions is itself flawed because the real objective should be to capture the proceeds flowing to landowners. Betterment levies and s106 require the developer to pass the costs on to landowners, but not always successfully.

The public-sector land purchase regime that was initiated after the Second World War, which underpinned the building of the new towns programme and local authority development, offered a substantively different approach. Because it was backed up with the threat of compulsory purchase, it removed the power of constraint available to landowners and went a long way towards dampening land speculation.

Enabling the public-sector once more to acquire land at prices close to its existing use value rather than its residential use value would bypass viability concerns while capturing all of the additional value for the state. This would open up the feasibility of a renewed public-sector building programme while minimising the upfront capital costs which arise from the cost of the land. It also, critically, provides a way of overcoming the ability of landowners to stall development by withholding land in the hope of higher returns at a future date.

3

The case for land reform

'Consider what rent is. It does not arise spontaneously from
land; it is due to nothing that the land owners have done.
It represents a value created by the whole community. Let
the land holders have, if you please, all that the possession
of the land would give them in the absence of the rest of the
community. But rent, the creation of the whole community,
necessarily belongs to the whole community.'

Henry George, 1879

We have so far described how land ownership impacts on
housebuilding, how land prices have risen to unprecedented
levels in recent decades and how previous governments
have tried, unsuccessfully, to claw back various proportions
of the increment arising from residential development. To
increase housebuilding output to the desired levels and,
crucially, to build more homes for the lower sections of
the market, requires reform of the land market. But before
we look at the kind of reform that might be necessary, we
should consider the moral case for doing so. Why shouldn't
the landowner be able to maximise their profit in the way
they currently can? What justification is there for incursions
into their existing rights?

The right to hold private property, after all, is fundamental
to capitalism. The ability to hold and exchange property

at a price agreed between a willing buyer and a willing seller is a cornerstone of the market economy and a liberal society. The feeling that property rights are sacrosanct, and that this extends to land tenure, is deeply embedded. The truth is, however, that the inclusion of land within this framework of inviolable property rights has not in the past been taken for granted so easily as it has been in recent decades. There have been economists and thinkers at many times who have questioned the idea of a private market in land. For the mid-twentieth century theorist Karl Polanyi, land was one of the three 'fictitious commodities' of the market economy (the others being labour and money). The marketisation, or commodification, of land was 'perhaps the weirdest of all the undertakings of our ancestors':

> The economic function is but one of many vital functions of land. It invests man's life with stability; it is the site of his habitation; it is a condition of his physical safety; it is the landscape and the seasons. We might as well imagine his being born without hands and feet as carrying on his life without land. And yet to separate land from man and to organize society in such a way as to satisfy the requirements of a real-estate market was a vital part of the utopian concept of a market economy.[1]

One does not need to reject the very existence of a market in land, however, to question the right of landowners to increases in land values resulting from the advance of the wider community. This, which should be at the heart of the contemporary housing debate, is a subject with which the classical economists were concerned. They identified that land, as a factor of production, had unique qualities with significant implications for the economy.

Specifically, land is fixed in supply and in location – it cannot be reproduced and it cannot be transported. This means that those who hold a particular piece of land control a monopoly. There are two objections that might be advanced to this argument. First, it can be said that in certain circumstances land is created by means of reclamation (from the sea, for example, as the Netherlands has done extensively). Second, it can be said that there are many different owners of land in competition with each other. These objections only help to clarify the difficulty, however, which is the value of a piece of land owing to its *location*. There is no way of creating more land within, say, five miles of Charing Cross. There is no way of creating more land within a five-minute walk from a newly-built train station. If you own land in those areas it will have a locational value owing to the productive activities of others, including taxpayer-funded works and services.

The classical economists and the theory of rent

The distinct nature of rent – as in the return to land – was addressed by Adam Smith, David Ricardo and John Stuart Mill in turn. Far from assuming that landowners were entitled to all of the profit from land they could make, all three argued or implied that such profit was in fact generated by the community. This line of thinking culminated politically in the attempt to introduce a land value tax in the 1909 'People's Budget'.

The underlying critique of land ownership was set out by Smith in *The Wealth of Nations* (1776), in which he described rent as a monopoly price which enabled the landowner to claim a share in the productive activities of the community without contributing anything himself to that process. If the eighteenth century tenant farmer improved his land, for example, the increase in income would ultimately be absorbed in higher rent. The same was true if the local population expanded and increased the demand for produce, or if roads and canals were installed that reduced transportation costs to the nearest town. In each case the additional profit that would be made by the farmer served to enhance the value of the land and therefore the rent, even though the landowner qua landowner played no part in these improvements. This meant that as the circumstances of society improved, the rent of the land would absorb an ever larger share of the improvements. As prices fell, saving the tenant money, the landowner would be able to raise the rent, leaving the tenant no better off:

> All those improvements in the productive powers of labour, which tend directly to reduce the real price of manufactures, tend indirectly to raise the real rent of land... Every increase in the real wealth of the society, every increase in the quantity of useful labour employed within it, tends indirectly to raise the real rent of land.[2]

Rent was 'naturally the highest which the tenant can afford to pay in the actual circumstances of the land' – that being all that is left for the farmer after paying for seed, labour, cattle and equipment, and the going profit for farming in the area.

> The rent of the land, therefore, considered as the price paid for the use of the land, is naturally a monopoly price. It is not at all proportioned to what the landlord may have laid out upon the improvement of the land, or to what he can afford to take; but to what the farmer can afford to give.[3]

Smith felt that ground rents were 'the species of revenue which can best bear to have a peculiar tax imposed upon them'. His views were modified and elaborated over the following century or so. From Ricardo's writings, particularly *On the Principles of Political Economy and Taxation* (1817), emerged the concept of economic rent, distinct from rent as the payment for the use of land. This was the surplus payment received by the owner for a factor of production above what is necessary to keep it in its present use: income accruing to the owner by virtue of their ownership and nothing more. It was derived not from the intrinsic value of the land but the use to which it could be put due its locational advantages. He reiterated Smith's view of rent as essentially extractive from the productive economy:

> The rise of rent is always the effect of the increasing wealth of the country, and of the difficulty of providing food for its augmented population. It is a symptom, but it is never a cause of wealth...[4]

Taking these ideas on, John Stuart Mill went further in explicitly challenging the 'sacredness' of property in land. It should not always be assumed that it be treated like any other item of property, he argued, because it had never been created by anybody and therefore nobody had a rightful claim to its ownership in the first place. Tracing back the title to a piece of land far enough would always lead to a case of expropriation, ultimately from the wider community. In his *Principles of Political Economy* (1848), Mill wrote:

> When the 'sacredness of property' is talked of, it should always be remembered, that any such sacredness does not belong in the same degree to landed property. No man made the land. It is the original inheritance of the whole species. Its appropriation is wholly a question of general expediency. When private property in land is not expedient, it is unjust.[5]

Mill also went further than Smith and Mill in proposing a response, calling in his later life for a tax on the future increments in land value. This proposal would not place a claim on values already accumulated, but only those generated henceforth. He justified it in remarks to the inaugural meeting of the Land Tenure Reform Association in 1871:

> Land is limited in quantity while the demand for it, in a prosperous country, is constantly increasing. The rent, therefore, and the price, which depends on the rent, progressively rises, not through the exertion or expenditure of the owner, to which we should not object, but by the mere growth of wealth and population. The incomes of landowners are rising while they are sleeping, through the general prosperity produced by the labour and outlay of other people.[6]

Building upon this tradition in the late nineteenth century was the American economist Henry George, whose *Progress and Poverty* (1879) depicted land hoarding, rent extraction and speculation on land values as the root of economic depressions, unemployment and poverty. In comments that echo various issues faced in the housing market today, George described the problem with landowners withholding land for speculative purposes:

> If I buy land for a small price and hold it until I can sell it for a large price, I have become rich, not by wages for my labor or by interest upon my capital, but by the increase in rent.[7]

For George, rent was the 'price of monopoly' arising from the individual ownership of natural elements that were irreproducible and upon which the rest of the community depended. As productive power increased, the owners of land would absorb more and more of the output in rent. George described three forces of material progress that drove up rent. The first was the general increase in population, and in particular what would today be called the agglomeration effects resulting from large numbers of people living near to each other. The second was improvements in productive processes, efficiencies and labour-saving machinery. The third was the very *expectation* that such material progress would continue to increase rents, thus encouraging the withholding of land from use in order to profit from future rent increases:

> ... the confident expectation of the future enhancement of land values, which arises in all progressive countries from the steady increase of rent... leads to speculation, or the holding of land for a higher price than it would otherwise then bring.[8]

This, he said, led to the effects of 'a combination among holders' who shared the same incentives, leading to the disuse of land in the hope of higher returns in the future:

> If the land of superior quality as to location were always fully used before land of inferior quality were resorted to, no vacant lots would be left as a city extended, nor would we find miserable shanties in the midst of costly buildings. These lots, some of them extremely valuable, are withheld from use, or from the full use to which they might be put, because their owners, not being able or not wishing to improve them, prefer, in expectation of the advance of land values, to hold them for a higher rate than could now be obtained from those willing to improve them.[9]

George became famous for his advocacy of 'the single tax': a 100 per cent tax on land values, which would enable all other taxes to be abolished. The effect of this would be for the private ownership of land to benefit no individual, with all of the profits collected by the state. This would achieve the same ends as the nationalisation of the land without the need for a change of ownership:

The great cause of inequality in the distribution of wealth is inequality in the ownership of land... to relieve labour and capital from all taxation, direct and indirect, and to throw the burden upon rent, would be, as far as it went, to counteract this tendency to inequality, and, if it went so far as to take in taxation the whole of rent, the cause of inequality would be totally destroyed.[10]

George became synonymous with the land reform movement of the late nineteenth century, his work inspiring the creation of numerous societies and groups that campaigned towards a land value tax. What pushed the issue of land and rent up the political agenda was not just the intellectual movement but two increasingly pressing practical considerations that threw the spotlight on the nature of land ownership. These were, firstly, the increasing costs of municipal improvements, which were resulting in higher levels of local taxation; and, secondly, concerns about land hoarding where land was in short supply for new homes.

Urbanisation and the 'conversion rent'

The theory of rent advanced by Smith and Ricardo dealt mainly with the returns to land in its agricultural use, that being still the predominant mode of economic activity in the late eighteenth and early nineteenth century. But that was rapidly changing, and the significance of their thought would in fact become much more obvious through the urbanisation that resulted from the Industrial Revolution. Industrialisation was accompanied not only by a population boom, which greatly increased the demand for land, but a concentration of that population in and around the major towns and cities, where work was most abundant. The number of English and Welsh towns numbering more than 20,000 inhabitants increased from 15 to 63 between 1801 and

1851. In the 1820s alone, Manchester, Birmingham, Sheffield and Leeds each grew by more than 40 per cent.[11]

This drove up the price of land suitable for housing in these locations, securing previously unimaginable windfalls for landowners who just happened to be in the right place at the right time. The rises in rent arising from gradual improvements in agricultural output, as described by Smith and Ricardo, were as nothing compared with this. The change of use from agricultural to residential resulted in enormous increases in the rent that could be charged by those landowners lucky enough to have witnessed the economic advance of the community around them. Offer (1981) calls this the 'conversion rent', adding: 'This was the great prize which urbanisation offered to the traditional owners of the land.'[12]

Even at the beginning of this period, the conversion of farmland to building land on the outskirts of Birmingham in the 1750s, for example, increased its value by between six and twelve times. Over the decades ahead, rents in those places where people most wanted (or needed) to live accelerated away from those that were economically less vibrant. By the turn of the twentieth century, an average working-class dwelling in London rented for about 70 per cent more than one in Birmingham and three times more than one in Macclesfield. The difference between some residential and agricultural land values was by then enormous: a built-up acre in the City of London attracted rent about four thousand times as much as an acre of farmland. A plot of land near the Bank of England was sold in 1905 for 32,500 times as much per acre than typical farmland.[13]

In his 1909 budget, David Lloyd George proposed a 20 per cent tax on the future increment of land and a tax (of a halfpenny in the pound) on the capital value of undeveloped, non-agricultural land. These were relatively timid measures that would not raise large amounts of money, as Lloyd George knew, but they had symbolic importance in opening a new front against the 'unearned increment'. Crucially, alongside these measures, there was to be a valuation of all land and it was this that opened up possibilities for more sweeping land taxation in the future. At a packed meeting in Limehouse, east London, in July 1909, Lloyd George made the case for the measures:

> Not far from here not so many years ago, between the Lea and the Thames, you had hundreds of acres of land which was not very useful even for agricultural purposes. In the main it was a sodden marsh. The commerce and the trade of London increased under free trade, the tonnage of your shipping went up by hundreds of thousands of tons and by millions, labour was attracted from all parts of the country to help with all this trade and business done here. What happened? There was no housing accommodation. This part of London became overcrowded and the population overflowed. That was the opportunity of the owners of the marsh. All that land became valuable building land, and land which used to be rented at £2 or £3 an acre has been selling within the last few years at £2,000 an acre, £3,000 an acre, £6,000 an acre, £8,000 an acre. Who created that increment? Who made that golden swamp? Was it the landlord? Was it his energy? Was it his brains, his forethought? It was purely the combined efforts of all the people engaged in the trade and commerce of that part of London – the trader, the merchant, the ship-owner, the dock labourer, the workman – everybody except the landlord.[14]

This was the culmination of several decades of increasing political pressure for a tax on land. It was motivated in part by the fact that, while landowners were collecting these enormous conversion rents by selling off their land for housing, the costs of the infrastructure needed to support that housing were mounting rapidly. Public works in the metropolis were necessary to alleviate the social problems resulting from the population surge from which landowners had profited. The urban population needed sewers, roads, lighting, police stations and schools.[15] In London, for instance, the Metropolitan Board of Works laid out large sums of money from the mid-1850s on the creation of the Chelsea and Victoria Embankments and the core of the capital's sewerage and drainage network. Funding for these works were all raised from local taxation, the 'rates' which were paid by tenants with some of the incidence probably falling on their landlords – as in the owners of houses, rather than the original landowners who had sold up at residential values. Rates rose as the decades went by, by thirty to fifty per cent in different parts of London between 1891 and 1906.

Landowners were profiting handsomely from the process of urbanisation, but the costs of it were being borne by working and middle-class tenants and the small-capitalist landlords who had at least invested in the construction of new housing.[16] This turned the relatively abstract theory of rent into a more immediate, tangible concern, driving it onto the political agenda in Westminster. The Liberals took up the cause on behalf of urban dwellers, capitalists and industry, all of whom lost out to the rising claims of rent. Effectively, the costs to towns and cities of industrialisation were being borne by workers and capitalists, but the rapid increases in land values were being accumulated by landowners. Liberal MP Harvey Lewis moved a Commons motion complaining that:

> ...those who had the strongest interest in metropolitan improvements were in reality those most free from taxation. In point of fact the taxation fell principally on the occupiers of

the metropolis, while the freeholders, who derived immense revenues from their property, scarcely paid anything.

In another parallel with today, pressure for reform was further motivated by concerns that landowners were stymying development by hoarding land to maximise their gains. Because the rates were a tax on the income received from property, disused sites were under-taxed if they were taxed at all, as they were generating little or no annual income. The issue of land-hoarding had been raised by the Royal Commission on the Housing of the Working Classes in 1884. This warned that the owners of land suitable for building had no financial incentive to release it quickly because they were taxed only on its current income rather than its much higher capital value:

> They can thus afford to keep their land out of the market, and to part with only small quantities, so as to raise the price beyond the natural monopoly price which the land would command by the advantages of its position. Meantime, the general expenditure of the town on improvements is increasing the value of their property.[17]

A Liberal leaflet in 1905 also accused landowners, 'by holding out for rents or prices which cannot be paid, are preventing the employment of workmen, the better housing of the people, and the expansion of all kinds of industry'.[18] Following this logic landowners were effectively profiting from the worsening conditions in the slums. In the months following the tax-raising 1909 budget, which provoked fury in the House of Lords leading ultimately to the constitutional crisis, ministers put the case to the country. Winston Churchill, then president of the Board of Trade, neatly encapsulated the arguments of Smith, Ricardo and Mill in his Edinburgh speech (quoted in the Introduction):

All goes back to the land, and the landowner... is enabled with resistless strength to absorb to himself a share of almost every public and every private benefit, however important or however pitiful those benefits may be.[19]

The taxes that emerged from the People's Budget raised very little money and had been scrapped, along with the valuation that was rolled out concurrently in hope of a more extensive land value tax, by 1920.[20] There was a further, abortive attempt to introduce a land value tax in 1931. In the post-war period the focus of policymakers shifted towards the idea of taxing betterment rather than an annual tax on site values.

Since the early twentieth century, the ideas of the classical economists regarding the unique character of land and its propensity to generate economic rent have been eased out of mainstream theory. As Ryan-Collins, Lloyd and Macfarlane (2017) write, neoclassical economics has tended not to draw a distinction between land and capital, despite their differences:

Despite the strong emphasis placed on land and its distinctive qualities by the classical economists, macroeconomics largely abandoned land as a separate topic for analysis... The standard aggregate 'production function' is made up simply of capital and labour with one substitutable for the other; land is absent. Land still features in microeconomic theory but as a factor of production with the same essential properties as capital or labour.[21]

Taxing land today

The case that was made for a land value tax in the nineteenth century is just as pertinent today. Land values are increasing, now like then, owing to the general increase in the population and rising wealth. This is generating returns for landowners (including today's homeowners) that are unearned. Those who own land which is ready to be switched from agricultural or industrial purposes to residential use stand to collect very substantial windfalls. Meanwhile the contributions of landowners and developers are often insufficient to cover the infrastructure requirements that arise from the development of new homes, the value of which is largely dependent on the public services and the community that they are in close proximity to.

In London today, for instance, there is evidence of a 'transport premium' of 10.5 per cent on the value of homes within 500 metres of an Underground or railway station, falling to 4.9 per cent at up to 1,000 metres distance and then nothing after 1,500 metres.[22] Those living in such locations today may already have paid for that premium in the purchase price, but at the point at which new stations are opened nearby landowners collect the windfall without having made any contribution to the work. KPMG and Savills have calculated that eight forthcoming Transport for London projects, such as Crossrail 2 and the extension of the Bakerloo line, could generate increases in land values of about £87 billion; the projects themselves will cost £36 billion.[23]

There have been, and there are still, advocates for a land value tax from across the political spectrum. On the free-market right, Milton Friedman called it 'the least bad tax'. The Institute of Economics Affairs endorsed the idea of a locational land value tax as recently as January 2017.[24] On the left, the Labour Party floated the idea in its 2017 general election manifesto. It is widely favoured by economists, as it was by the independent Mirrlees Review of 2010/11 which said the case for a land value tax was 'very strong':

Taxing land ownership is equivalent to taxing an economic rent – to do so does not discourage any desirable activity. Land is not a produced input; its supply is fixed and cannot be affected by the introduction of a tax.

Because the supply of land would be unchanged, people would not pay more for it and so the tax would be capitalised into land prices – the increase in the tax would result in a corresponding fall in the value of the land, so that the incidence would be on landowners rather than the economic activity that takes place on it. Thus it could be imposed 'at an arbitrarily high rate on economic efficiency grounds'.[25]

Despite sound economic logic supporting the idea of a land value tax, there are practical difficulties to its implementation, including for example the disaggregation of the value of the land from the value of any buildings upon it. Because there are relatively few transactions in land – separate to the property situated on it – it is difficult to determine the market price in order to apply any tax consistently. This, as Mirrlees pointed out, need not matter from an efficiency point of view, but if valuations were not accurate then there would be 'inequities between taxpayers'.[26] These are not insurmountable problems, however. The Greater London Assembly's Planning Committee has called for an economic feasibility study and a trial of a land value tax in the capital, pointing out that it would discourage land-banking and encourage the more efficient use of land.[27]

The biggest obstacle to the introduction of a land value tax – and perhaps why it has failed to be introduced in the past – is probably political. Quite apart from the fact that it would involve introducing 'another tax', there would be a large number of losers, including millions of homeowners in the South-East of England, who would object to it. There would be a large number of winners too, and there would be a clear argument on equity grounds if it was introduced to replace the council tax, which is highly-regressive (the more the property is worth, the less as a proportion of the value is paid). But the trade-off would be difficult for the government. When Labour promised in May 2017 merely to initiate a review considering such a shift it was written off by the Conservatives as a 'garden tax' that would hit 10 million householders.[28]

Capturing the 'conversion rent'

Another way of taxing land is to levy a charge on the increase in value that comes with a change of use. Rather than an annual charge on the rental value of land, as with a land value tax, this would be a one-off levy on the capital value capturing the windfall gain when the designated use of a piece of land changes. In particular this can be used to tax the increase that arises from permission to use land for housing, which usually results in a very large windfall for the owner. This would be much more straightforward than a land value tax, would not impact on existing homeowners and yet would raise substantial sums of money.

This is, of course, what was attempted at various points during the post-war decades with limited success, as described in Chapter 2. These each failed because of the ability of landowners to sit out the policy and wait for it to be repealed. The key difference between a betterment levy such as was repeatedly attempted and a land value tax is in its effect on supply. The latter, levied annually, would not affect the supply of land; a betterment levy, however, is dependent on an action being taken by the owner. This creaties an incentive for the owner not to take the action (bringing the land forward for housing development) that would trigger the incursion of the levy. As Mirrlees pointed out, each attempt at a betterment tax failed 'in large part as a result of the lack of credibility over the long-term sustainability of the tax. There has been a clear incentive to wait for a reversal of the policy before applying for planning permission'.[29]

But waiting for a reversal of policy was not an option that was available to the owners of land that was purchased by public authorities at existing use value in the late 1940s and 1950s. This approach achieved the same end of collecting the increase in value for the state, but by way of prior ownership rather than a tax. It also removed any requirement for calculating the locational value of the land separate from the structures. The merits of this approach were extolled in the 1942 Uthwatt Report:

> In the case of recoupment... the authority buy outright the land likely to be enhanced in value by their proposed works, paying the owner its current market value, and any profit they are able to make by developing or selling it is entirely theirs; there is, therefore, no need to ascertain how much of the profit is attributable to increase in value to particular works and how much to other causes, and the major difficulty of the existing betterment system is avoided.[30]

This was the mechanism used in the development of the new towns, where land was purchased at its existing use value, with future rents and land sales to commercial developers providing a valuable income stream over the following years. It was also used by local authorities for the redevelopment of town centres and the construction of council housing. It has also been used around the world, including much of Europe, including Germany, the Netherlands and France, where it has not only enabled the acquisition of land at lower prices but in doing so has doused price-inflating speculation generally.

In the Netherlands, for instance, an Expropriation Act empowered authorities to purchase land in an 'approved extension area' at the value of the land in its current use:

> For decades most Dutch municipalities customarily have bought land a few years in advance of development, prepared it for development, and then sold or leased the actual development sites, retaining a substantial portion of the land for roads, parks and community facilities. In the Netherlands, the long experience of municipal land acquisition of the urban-extension type has so affected expectations that speculation in development land is considerably restricted.[31]

In France a similar approach has been used for the acquisition of larger areas of development. This 'dampens the grosser excesses of speculation while leaving the bulk of land transaction in private hands'.[32]

Conclusion

There are strong arguments for taxing increases in land values ahead of much else. As the classical economists set out, rising locational value is an unearned income. The source of that unearned income is not just the advance of the wider community but specific public investments in infrastructure, such as roads, sewerage, public services and so on, all of which increase the amenity of housing in the local area and without which the land would be very much less desirable and therefore commanding lower values.

But introducing a tax on all land on an annual basis in the form of a land value tax faces large political obstacles. A narrower tax focusing only on the very considerable increase in value that accrues to a small number of landowners when planning permission is granted is attractive on the same principles and has been attempted on various occasions in the past in the guise, for example, of a development charge and a betterment levy (see Chapter 2). But such a tax is always impeded by the landowner's ability to sit out such a policy and bring development to a halt.

A different way of achieving the same end would be to remove from landowners their ability to withhold land in pursuit of more favourable circumstances and a higher sale price at some point in the future. This could be achieved by enabling the public sector to purchase land that is designated for new housing at close to its existing use value – that is, without regard to the prospective planning permission that it might receive. This power might be wielded by local authorities, development corporations, combined authorities or the Mayor of London. Where utilised, this would enable the public sector to purchase land, grant itself planning permission and then either sell it to developers at its residential value, thereby collecting the increase for the state, or keeping it in public ownership to generate a permanent revenue stream and/or to provide affordable accommodation at much less cost than currently.

4

Where do we go from here?

'I do not think that the man who makes money by unearned increment in land is morally worse than anyone else who gathers his profit where he finds it in this hard world under the law and according to common usage. It is not the individual I attack; it is the system. It is not the man who is bad; it is the law which is bad. It is not the man who is blameworthy for doing what the law allows and what other men do; it is the State which would be blameworthy if it were not to endeavour to reform the law and correct the practice.'

Winston Churchill, 1909

The challenge for policymakers in housing is to ensure that more homes are built in the places where we need them most and – crucially – in the right mix. The failure of housing supply does not just lie in an overall shortfall of numbers but in a lack of new homes for less expensive sections of the market, and of sub-market provision. There are some who suggest that the mix of new homes is unimportant, because all additional units increase supply in the aggregate and that a process of 'filtering' means there are beneficial knock-on effects all the way through the market. This would be a more convincing argument if supply was already keeping up with projected household formation. But it isn't, and this is because the homes that are built are targeted overwhelmingly at the higher ends of the market. Where prices are highest and homes are most needed – including much of London and the South East – only one in five households can afford the average new-build.[1] The unbalanced mix of homes being built, with a narrow audience of potential buyers, is itself a barrier to higher levels of output. For homes to be built in greater quantities, they need to be affordable to a wider range of households.

The land market is not responding to this. This is partly a question of planning constraints, but there are significant quantities of potential housing land that do have planning permission that are not being brought forward and then developed at the rate that is required. There is a simple reason for this: the greatest financial rewards for landowners lie in a patient drip-feed of supply for higher-end developments. Meanwhile, the provision of sub-market housing via developer contributions is declining as the Section 106 process is being gamed for the same reasons. The focus of housing supply reform needs to be on ensuring more land is brought forward more quickly and at values that are consistent with faster building and a broader mix of supply.

The challenge is to create new financial incentives that push in a different direction, discouraging landowners from withholding land from the purposes for which the community needs it to be put. Also required is a reassessment of how sub-market homes are delivered. Their provision needs to be less reliant on capricious private-sector development, and more on enhanced public-sector funding. As of late 2017, there were various housing initiatives that showed promise but which still so far faced considerable uncertainty in implementation.

Theresa May announced to the 2017 Conservative conference that the government would be encouraging councils to build homes again. This had been billed by Damian Green, first secretary of state, earlier in the day as the 'rebirth of council housing'.[2] In fact, local authorities are only being invited to bid for funds, with housing associations, from an affordable housing budget enlarged from £7 billion to £9 billion. But it indicated a willingness on the part of the government to increase council housebuilding once more and to ensure, as was part of the announcement, that the construction of genuinely-affordable social rented housing will be stepped up again.

Even if ministers wanted to return to the local authority housebuilding levels of the 1950s and 1960s, when council output was usually well above 100,000 a year, there is the issue of cost to overcome. On the basis of the £80,000 subsidy quoted by the Department for Communities and Local Government as the cost of a new home for social rent, 100,000 annually would cost £8 billion a year – almost the same per year as the government currently plans to spend on the affordable housing budget for the duration of the parliament.[3] Given the high and rising housing benefit costs that are required to help people pay market rents they cannot afford, there is a strong case for investing upfront in subsidised accommodation. Capital Economics has calculated that increased investment in social housing investment would create a net surplus for the state by the mid-2030s, adding: 'The economic and fiscal case for building new social rent housing is unanswerable.'[4]

But this requires a long-term perspective of the public finances. It requires the present government to increase borrowing now to allow a government 20 years hence to reap the fiscal reward. It would be the right thing to do, but it is at odds with the fiscal straitjacket the Conservatives have imposed on themselves since 2010 and will become increasingly less palatable to the chancellor if the public finances continue to show little sign of substantial improvement.[5] The obvious thing to do would be to remove the caps on local authority's housing revenue accounts, enabling them to borrow to invest in new homes, but this has been repeatedly rejected by the government.[6]

Meanwhile the communities secretary, Sajid Javid, is spearheading reform of the planning system to make it more responsive to the need for additional housing. The housing white paper in February 2017 proposed a new delivery test that would hold local authorities to account for an under-supply of homes in their areas. The government is also working up a new standardised methodology for assessing need, to ensure that local authorities are planning for the right number of homes. This, significantly, will take affordability into account as well as projected household growth. Under plans put out for consultation in late 2017, areas with median house prices that are more than four times median earnings will be expected to increase their housing targets above and beyond their baseline demographic forecasts, a methodology that will bring England's estimated total housing need up to 266,000 homes a year, including 72,000 in London.[7] The government has been less forthright when it comes to the green belt, even though there is a clear case for at least reviewing boundaries that were set down more than 60 years ago, and when the decision to restrict the growth of cities was accompanied by meaningful efforts to provide for 'overspill' in a network of new towns.

Nevertheless, the reforms that are in view will increase the pressure on councils to approve more homes in the places where prices are highest. What they will not ensure is that those homes will be built. The biggest weakness of the 2017 housing white paper was that it failed to deal with issues of market absorption that, as described in Chapter 1, emanate from the rational profit-maximising behaviour of landowners. There is a power of constraint in the land market that needs to be overcome.

One of the most innovative plans to increase the provision of affordable housing has come from City Hall, which believes there is a need in London for 50 per cent of output to be 'genuinely affordable' (it was only 13 per cent in 2015/16). To that end, the Mayor of London has published new planning guidance designed to ensure that private schemes comprise at least 35 per cent affordable units. This will be incentivised by a new procedure under which schemes that meet the 35 per cent threshold will be fast-tracked through the planning process, while those that do not will be subject to detailed interrogation, potentially in public, to establish where the profit is going instead. The idea is to encourage developers only to bid for land at prices that reflect the 35 per cent threshold and thereby 'embed' affordable housing requirements into land values in the capital.[8] If successful, this is a model that could potentially be used more widely (although the stipulated threshold would have to reflect local market conditions). There is one question-mark hanging over the idea, however, and that is whether landowners will play ball in a framework in which they are being asked to accept lower prices for their sites.

Further reform
What is required is a reform that ensures that the land market consistently releases the land that is required for housing requirements and planning objectives to be met, and that reduces the cost of land for publicly-funded housebuilding. There is a single reform that would deliver

both of these things, and that is to remove from landowners the entitlement they currently have to future increases in value arising from a prospective change of use – such as the granting of residential planning permission. This is the key to shifting the financial incentives facing landowners and removing from them the power of constraint they have over development that is in the interests of the community. As well be explore in more detail below, it requires reform of the Land Compensation Act 1961, which enshrines their right to receive 'hope value' – that arising from the hope of future development – in addition to any current use value in the event of compulsory purchase by the state.

The effect would be to give public authorities the power once more to acquire land at prices closer to its current use value rather than its potential residential use value. This would reframe incentives in the operation of the land market. The alternative to settling for lower bids for land would no longer be to wait a little longer; it would be to lose the land to the state at even less profit. The incentive for the landowner in such a scenario would be to settle more quickly. This would provide the ultimate sanction against the withholding of land from uses to which local authorities wish it to be put, and instead ensure that it is brought forward at prices compatible with planning objectives – including the provision of substantial numbers of sub-market homes and the infrastructure that local people rightly expect.

There would be major fiscal advantages too. Local authorities and development corporations would be able to buy agricultural land at tens of thousands of pounds per hectare and then either sell on plots at residential values (often millions per hectare) to builders, raising large amounts of money to use as they see fit, or use the land to build council homes, vastly reducing the upfront cost of doing so. In inner-cities they would be able to acquire brownfield sites at something close to industrial value – more expensive than in agricultural use but still only in the hundreds of thousands per hectare.

Note that there would be no need for the large-scale compulsory acquisition of land. That would not be desirable and it is not what is intended. While public authorities would have to be prepared to use it if necessary, the practical effect would be to encourage landowners to settle for lower sums without forcing local authorities to resort to compulsory-purchase proceedings which they (landowners) would in any case lose. There is no reason why councils could not offer a modest premium to landowners, but that should be proportionate to the land in its existing use rather than its residential use. Where implemented, this would provide a comprehensive alternative to the current system of developer contributions. Unlike the Section 106 process, it could at the same time raise substantial sums for public works, remove uncertainty for developers and pass the costs on to landowners.

Such a regime could be applied in various ways. It could be used simply as a backstop to ensure that land is forthcoming at values consistent with planning objectives, such as the Mayor of London's requirement for new developments to comprise 35 per cent affordable units. It could be used to capture the increase in land values arising from specific transport projects, such as Crossrail 2, extensions to the Tube and Docklands Light Railway, and planned investment in the East West Corridor linking Oxford, Milton Keynes and Cambridge.[9] Or it could be used more extensively as a tool for building a national land bank, with the windfall profits generated by all future development land accruing to the public purse.

Improving housing supply

In the short term the application of this approach could be applied incrementally in those areas with the greatest pressures on housing in order to improve not just the quantity but the mix of new homes. These could be designated as Special Housing Zones in which the local authority, a combined authority or the Mayor of London, would have the power to acquire land at values that do not include prospective planning permission. This land could then be used for social or affordable housing directly commissioned by the authority. Or it could be sold on to builders for market sale with conditions attached concerning the rate of build and how much they are to be sold for (these conditions being reflected in the residential value that builders attach to the land).

The government's proposed new methodology for assessing housing need may provide a potential framework for such an approach: those areas where prices are most out of sync with local earnings are to be required to increase their housing targets relative to their projected household formation. But, as noted already, simply approving more land for development is unlikely to ensure that it is built, and especially in those areas that are most expensive already. Designating those areas as Special Housing Zones and using the framework outlined here would enable housing output to be stepped up in areas where prices are highest and where output is most constrained by the aspirational demands of landowners.

Another approach would be to use it to open up new areas, particularly in the South-East, to fresh development in the form of new towns and garden cities. Again, designating an area of land as a Special Housing Zone and enabling a development corporation to acquire the requisite sites at close to agricultural use value. New developments could be master-planned with infrastructure installed upfront and the costs earned back from the sale of plots to developers, smaller builders and even self-builders at residential values.

Where there is a case for building on the green belt, by initiating swaps for instance, then a Special Housing Zone should again be designated and the land purchased by the local authority or a development corporation at close to its existing use value. If the profits arising from such a development were reinvested in the community, this would be one way of persuading local communities to accept development that they might otherwise oppose.

Current land debate

The cost of land in the housebuilding process has been increasingly of interest to policymakers and campaigners across the political spectrum. This has led to a raft of suggestions that the public sector should once again purchase land at values that do not reflect its potential residential use so that development can be undertaken more cheaply. The homelessness charity Shelter has drawn up proposals for 'New Civic Housebuilding' which is built around the idea of obtaining land at 'fair values' in order to produce high-quality developments.[10] The Centre for Progressive Capitalism has advocated land value capture as a means of increasing infrastructure spending which would open up new areas for housebuilding.[11] On the free-market right, the Adam Smith Institute has called for the government to raise money by letting councils 'buy land, grant it planning permission, and then sell it off, increasing its value many times'.[12] Centre-right commentators including Tim Montgomerie and Allister Heath have also argued the difference in value between agricultural and residential land could be used to invest in housing and/or infrastructure.[13] [14] Kate Barker, who led the seminal 2004 review of housing, recently urged the government 'to be more interventionist in the land market, in terms of acquiring land for new towns or big urban extensions'.[15]

At the 2017 general election, both main parties stood on manifestos promising some degree of land value capture. The Conservatives pledged to 'work with private and public sector house builders to capture the increase in land value created when they build to reinvest in local infrastructure, essential services and further housing, making it both easier and more certain that public sector landowners, and communities themselves, benefit from the increase in land value from urban regeneration and development'.[16] A press briefing during the campaign separately described the government's intention to 'allow councils to buy brownfield land and pocket sites more cheaply'.[17] The government has already taken tentative steps in this direction. The Neighbourhood Planning Act, which received Royal Assent just before the 2017 general election, gave local authorities the power to set up new town development corporations which could purchase land for new garden towns and villages. This improved the scope for local authorities to create new developments from scratch, at some distance from the objections of residents in the suburbs of existing conurbations, and with commitments to infrastructure and affordable housing guaranteed from an early stage in the planning.

What is currently lacking, however, is the ability of any public-sector body to purchase land for new homes at anything less than residential value – whether that land has planning permission or not. This is a critical point and lies at the nub of the housing supply issue today.

Land compensation rules

It is not enough to suggest that land could be acquired more cheaply simply by purchasing it before planning permission is granted. This might be possible with public land. But private land is released incrementally and deliberately at the rate that will maximise the windfall for the owner; if that means waiting a while, then in the current legal framework that option is always there and the landowner usually has little to lose by pursuing it. A local authority submitting an offer for a piece of land intended for housing but priced at anything less than its residential value would simply be rebuffed by a rational owner. Landowners (apart from a small minority of philanthropically-inclined individuals) do not tend to voluntarily part with their land for less than they could achieve currently on the open market.

That the land does not yet have planning permission does not substantially affect this situation. Land that is suitable for housing and has any chance of being included in a development plan will already have 'hope value' – that from the hope that the land will in future be used, in our example, for residential development. It may even have been traded at this higher value already.

Moreover, as described above, the right of a landowner to hold out for residential value is enshrined in the 1961 Land Compensation Act, which made clear that compensation should take account of all the potentialities of the land acquired – including its potential for development.[18] The Act states, specifically, that the value of the land is 'taken to be the amount which the land if sold in the open market by a willing seller might be expected to realise'. That may take account of planning permission that is either already received or – crucially – 'could reasonably have been expected to be granted' at a later date. If the local authority intends that the land be used for housing, then the sum to be paid will reflect its residential value, irrespective of whether planning permission is already in place.

The 1961 Act, therefore, did not only guarantee the landowner the right to the value of the land at the use to which it was already being put, it also guaranteed the right to any hope value arising from a prospective future planning permission. The effect of this has been to encourage speculation, hoarding and incremental development.

The reality of the present legal framework is sometimes obscured by the fact that compensation for compulsory purchase is also meant to be set at the market value in the absence of the scheme for which the purchase is being made; this is the no-scheme world, or Pointe Gourde, principle.[19] The 1961 Act also specifically provides for new town designation to be disregarded when compensation is being calculated. These two provisions can lead to the assumption that the public sector can in fact purchase land for homes at less than its residential value, but this is mistaken.

These exemptions only exclude the value that *those specific developments* to be undertaken as a result of the compulsory purchase would create. They do not override any reasonable expectation of profit that may already obtain in the no-scheme world. For example, if a local authority or a development corporation wished to compulsorily-purchase a piece of land for new homes, then under the no-scheme world rule the valuation for compensation should disregard the additional value arising from that specific project. However, if the land *already* had any reasonable prospect of future development for housing (irrespective of the scheme under consideration) then that *would* be reflected in the valuation.

Thus when industrial land was acquired under compulsory purchase powers for the Olympic Park in East London, landowner Rooff claimed that they should have been compensated at residential use value on the basis that that land might at some point have been used for housing. After a lengthy legal battle, the landowner won.[20] As the law stands then, local authorities are unable to purchase land at its existing use value, or indeed anything less than its full residential value. In order to enable that, the government would have to reform the land compensation rules to stipulate that market values do not reflect any prospective or hoped-for planning permission.

Conclusion

Reforming the land compensation rules in the way described would facilitate a radical new departure in housing supply. It would enable planning objectives to be imposed, for affordable housing to be built in greater quantities and for infrastructure to be provided where it is needed. It would bypass the need for negotiated developer contributions that deliver less and less and become a cause of delay, and it would ensure that the cost is borne by landowners rather than builders. With the promise of sufficient infrastructure, local concerns about the impact of development on local amenities could be allayed. A new generation of new towns would present the opportunity to bypass the difficulties currently associated with the piecemeal, sequential, speculative developments on the outskirts of towns and cities. New developments could be master-planned and would provide greater scope for land to be broken up for small builders and self-builders who often struggle to get a foothold in the land market.

Politically, the main parties have already been looking in

this direction. In the 2017 general election the Conservative manifesto pledged to 'reform Compulsory Purchase Orders to make them easier and less expensive for councils to use and to make it easier to determine the true market value of sites'. Labour, in a housing 'mini-manifesto', promised to increase local authority powers including 'enabling compulsory purchase at a price closer to existing value'. While neither party won an outright majority, between them they won 82.4 per cent of the vote and 580 out of 650 seats. They now need to see the reform through.

Conclusion

The challenge of improving housing supply is not a straightforward one. Against most measures of need, total output needs to be substantially increased. But within that increase needs to be a disproportionately large rise in the number of homes that are built for the less expensive sections of the market, and for the sub-market social sector too. These are not separate issues: concentrating building on higher-end sales brings with it market absorption difficulties that limit overall output. Only by ensuring that development caters to a broad cross-section of the market, and by building subsidised social housing too, will the right homes be built in sufficient quantities where we need them most. The current housebuilding model is unequal to this challenge. In those areas where housing costs are most expensive – such as London – output is most geared towards the higher reaches of the market.

This is a function of the land market and it is there that reform needs to be focused if we are to build the homes we need and bring down housing costs in the long run. Landowners, behaving rationally in the institutional framework they find themselves in, have a power of constraint over development that is at odds with the interests of the wider community. Reforming the land compensation rules, and enabling local authorities to purchase land at prices that do not reflect prospective planning permission, would loosen up the land market, prevent hoarding and douse speculation. By rewiring incentives for landowners, it would help private-sector developers obtain land at prices that would enable them to build the kind of homes in the kind of timeframes desired by local planning authorities. And where the power was utilised by the local authority it would have large fiscal benefits, enabling town halls to either build council homes more cheaply or to collect the increase in values from selling sites on to market builders.

There are good reasons for protecting private property from the overweening state, but the windfalls that landowners are collecting by exercising their right to withhold land are unearned and detrimental to the country's housing objectives. If we want housing development to follow the course that is required then we will need to challenge their right to do that.

Notes

Introduction

1 Quoted in *The Times*, 17 July 1909
2 Ibid
3 Adam Smith, *The Wealth of Nations*, 1776, Bk.1, Ch.11
4 Katharina Knoll, Moritz Schularick and Thomas Steger, 'No Price Like Home: Global House Prices, 1870-1912', Centre for Economic Policy Research, September 2014
5 DCLG Table 563 (discontinued since 2010)
6 Centre for Progressive Capitalism, 'Estimating land value capture for England – updated analysis', March 2017

1   Housebuilding and the role of land

1 Nigel Henretty, 'Housing affordability in England and Wales: 1997 to 2016', Office of National Statistics, 17 March 2017
2 English Housing Survey, FT1101
3 Speech to Conservative Party Conference, 2017
4 Oxford Economics, 'Forecasting UK house prices and home ownership', November 2016
5 'English Housing Survey 2015 to 2016: housing costs and affordability'
6 'New OECD Affordable Housing Database', http://www.oecd.org/social/affordable-housing-database.htm [accessed 16 October 2017]
7 Outturn and forecast, Spring Budget 2017
8 Danielle Ryan, 'Statutory homelessness and prevention and relief, April to June (Q2) 2017: England', DCLG
9 DCLG, '2014-based Household Projections: England, 2014-2039', July 2016
10 Kate Barker, 'Review of Housing Supply, Final Report – Recommendations', HMSO, 2004, p.5

11 Evidence to House of Lords Select Committee on Economic Affairs, December 2015
12 House of Lords Select Committee on Economic Affairs, 'Building more homes', July 2016
13 DCLG, 'Fixing our broken housing market', February 2017
14 DCLG, 'Housing supply: net additional dwellings, England: 2015-16', November 2016
15 Daniel Bentley, 'Housing supply and household growth, national and local', Civitas, December 2016
16 Neal Hudson, 'Measuring housing need', Savills, January 2015
17 Savills, 'Planning to solve the housing crisis', 2017
18 Daniel Bentley, 'Planning approvals vs housebuilding activity, 2006-2015', Civitas, August 2016
19 Shelter, 'Planning permissions, completions and profits', July 2017
20 OFT, 'Homebuilding in the UK: A market study', September 2008, pp.118-119
21 Nathaniel Lichfield & Partners, 'Start to Finish: How quickly do large-scale housing sites deliver?', November 2016
22 Evidence to House of Commons Communities and Local Government Select Committee, 31 October 2016
23 Tom Archer and Ian Cole, 'Profits before Volume? Major housebuilders and the crisis of housing supply', Sheffield Hallam University, October 2016
24 Molior, 'Barriers to Housing Delivery', GLA, 2012, p.9
25 Nathaniel Lichfield and Partners, 'Stock and Flow: Planning Permissions and Housing Output', January 2017
26 Pat McAllister, Emma Street, Pete Wyatt, 'Shovel Ready? An empirical investigation of stalled residential sites', Henley Business School, University of Reading, November 2013
27 Robert A. Grovenstein, James B. Kau, Henry J. Munneke, 'Development Value: A Real Options Approach Using Emperical Data', *The Journal of Real Estate Finance and Economics*, October 2011
28 Peijun Guo, 'Private real estate investment analysis within a one-shot decision framework', *International Real Estate Review*, 2010
29 Sheridan Titman, 'Urban Land Prices Under Uncertainty', *The American Economic Review*, 1985
30 Laura Quigg, 'Empirical Testing of Real Option-Pricing Models', Journal of Finance, 1993
31 David Adams, 'Compulsory sale orders as a response to hardcore urban vacancy and dereliction', presented at University of Sheffield, 2015

32 DCLG Table 120
33 McAllister et al (2013)
34 Outer London Commission, 'Sixth Report: Removing the barriers to housing delivery', March 2016
35 Shelter, 'Planning permissions, completions and profits', July 2017
36 Katy Warrick and Edward Green, 'London needs more affordably priced homes', Savills, 2017
37 Mayor of London, 'London Housing Strategy, Draft for Public Consultation', September 2017
38 Ibid
39 Stephen Merrett, *State housing in Britain*, Routledge & Kegan Paul, 1979, p.24
40 Stephen Inwood, *City of Cities: The Birth of Modern London*, Macmillan, 2005, pp.184-185
41 *The Times*, 19 April 1913
42 *Hansard*, 17 February 1914
43 Merrett, *State housing in Britain*, p.61 and p.320
44 Peter Malpass and Alan Murie, Housing Policy and Practice (5th edition), Palgrave, 1999, p.58
45 DCLG Live Table 1012
46 DCLG Live Table 104
47 Outturn and forecast, Spring Budget 2017
48 Justin Chaloner, Alexandra Dreisin, Mark Pragnell, 'Building New Social Rent Homes', Capital Economics, June 2015

2   Land values and where they go

1 DCLG, 'Land value estimates for policy appraisal', December 2015
2 Centre for Progressive Capitalism, 'Estimating land value capture for England – updated analysis', March 2017
3 Christian Hilber and Wouter Vermeulen, 'The impact of supply constraints on house prices in England', *The Economic Journal*, June 2015
4 John Muellbauer, 'When is a Housing Market Overheated Enough to Threaten Stability?', University of Oxford Discussion Papers, September 2012
5 Oxford Economics, 'Forecasting UK house prices and home ownership', November 2016
6 Barry Cullingworth and Vincent Nadin, *Town and country planning in the UK*, Routledge, 2006, pp.22-23
7 Ibid, p.18

8   *Hansard*, 29 January 1947
9   Andrew Cox, *Adversary politics and land*, Cambridge University Press, 1984, p.94 and 97
10 Cullingworth and Nadin, p.197
11 Cox, p.109
12 Owen Connellan, *Land Value Taxation in Britain*, Lincoln Institute of Land Policy, 2004, p.7
13 *The Times*, 8 August 1958
14 Author's calculations from Table 244
15 *Hansard*, 1 December 1952
16 TCPA, 'New Towns and Garden Cities: Lessons for Tomorrow', 2014
17 Department of Planning Oxford Brookes University, 'Transferable Lessons from the New Towns', DCLG, 2006
18 TCPA, 'New Towns and Garden Cities: Lessons for Tomorrow', 2014
19 Connellan, p.8
20 Merrett, p.73
21 Cox, p.114
22 Cox, p.119
23 DCLG Table 563
24 Merrett, p.153 (real-terms calculations using ONS CPI data)
25 Merrett, p.71
26 Connellan, pp.8-10 and 13
27 Cox, p.88
28 V.H. Blundell, 'Labour's Flawed Land Acts 1947-1976', Economic and Social Science Research Association, 1993
29 Malcolm Grant, 'Compensation and Betterment', in Barry Cullingworth, British Planning, The Athlone Press, 1999, p.69ff Conclusion
30 Ibid, p.71
31 McAllister et al (2013)
32 'Contributing To Sustainable Communities – A New Approach To Planning Obligations', Statement By The Office Of The Deputy Prime Minister, 30 January 2004
33 Barker, p.67
34 Grant, p.69ff
35 Ibid, p.75
36 McAllister et al (2013)
37 RICS, 'Financial Viability Appraisal in Planning Decisions: Theory and Practice', April 2015
38 Ibid
39 Sarah Sayce et al, 'Viability and the Planning System: The Relationship between Economic Viability Testing, Land Values and Affordable Housing in London', January 2017

40 Ibid
41 Ibid
42 Pat McAllister, Edward Shepherd, Pete Wyatt, 'Policy shifts, developer contributions and land value capture in London 2005-2017', University of Reading (publication forthcoming)
43 Sayce et al
44 Association for Public Service Excellence, 'Building homes, creating communities: Ensuring councils provide innovative solutions to meeting housing need', p.38
45 Christine Whitehead et al, 'Delivering affordable housing through Section 106: outputs and outcomes', Joseph Rowntree Foundation, May 2006
46 Liz Peace et al, 'A New Approach to Developer Contributions: A Report by The CIL Review Team', DCLG
47 The University of Sheffield, Opinion Research Services, Hannah Hickman Consulting, 'Attitudinal research on financial payments to reduce opposition to new homes', DCLG, July 2017
48 DCLG, 'Fixing our broken housing market', February 2017

3   The case for land reform

1   Karl Polanyi, *The Great Transformation*, Beacon Press, 2001, p.187
2   Adam Smith, *The Wealth of Nations*, Bk.1, Ch.11
3   Adam Smith, *The Wealth of Nations*, Bk.1, Ch.11
4   David Ricardo, *On the Principles of Political Economy and Taxation*, Ch.2
5   John Stuart Mill, *Principles of Political Economy with some of their Applications to Social Philosophy*, 1848, Bk.II, Ch.II
6   Quoted in Avner Offer, *Property and Politics 1870-1914*, Cambridge University Press, 1981, p.183
7   Henry George, *Progress and Poverty*, Robert Schalkenbach Foundation, 1935 p.166
8   Ibid, p.255
9   Ibid, p.257
10 Ibid, p.311
11 M.E. Rose, 'Social change and the industrial revolution', in *The Economic History of Britain Since 1700*, Vol. I, Roderick Floud and Donald McCloskey (eds.), Cambridge University Press, 1981
12 Offer, p.114
13 Ibid, p.255
14 *The Times*, 31 July 1909
15 Offer, p.177

16 Ibid, p.231
17 Quoted in Offer, p.186
18 Quoted in Offer, p.318
19 *The Times*, 17 July, 1909
20 Cox, p.30
21 Josh Ryan-Collins, Toby Lloyd, Laurie Macfarlane, *Rethinking the Economics of Land and Housing*, Zed Books, 2017, pp.50-51
22 'London homebuyers willing to pay a substantial premium to live near a Tube or train station'. Nationwide Building Society, 2014
23 'Land value capture', Transport for London, February 2017
24 Rory Meakin, 'Reforming Britain's tax system', Institute of Economic Affairs, January 2017
25 James Mirrlees et al, *Tax by design*, Institute for Fiscal Studies, September 2011, p.371
26 Mirrlees et al, p.375
27 'Tax Trial: A land value tax for London?', London Assembly Planning Committee, February 2016
28 Ben Riley-Smith, 'Labour's garden tax will hit 10 million households', *The Daily Telegraph*, 4 June 2017
29 Mirrlees et al, p.372
30 Quoted in Connellan, p.70
31 Ibid, p.70
32 Ibid, p.69

4 Where do we go from here?

1 Savills, 'On track to solve the housing crisis?', October 2017
2 Jessica Elgot, 'Theresa May to unveil plan for "rebirth" in council housing in conference speech' *The Guardian*, 4 October 2017
3 DCLG, '£2 billion boost for affordable housing and long term deal for social rent', 4 October 2017
4 Justin Chaloner, Alexandra Dreisin, Mark Pragnell, 'Building New Social Rent Homes', Capital Economics, June 2015
5 Ben Chu, 'Philip Hammond expected to forecast "nasty" outlook for UK public finances', *The Independent*, 5 October 2017
6 DCLG, 'Government Response to the Communities and Local Government Select Committee Report: Capacity in the Homebuilding Industry', October 2017
7 DCLG, 'Planning for the right homes in the right places: consultation proposals', September 2017

8   Mayor of London, 'Homes for Londoners: Affordable housing and viability supplementary planning guidance 2017', August 2017

9   Thomas Aubrey, 'Funding the Infrastructure and Affordable Housing for the East West Corridor', Centre for Progressive Capitalism, October 2017

10 Shelter, 'New Civic Housebuilding: Rediscovering our tradition of building beautiful and affordable homes', 2017

11 Thomas Aubrey, 'Bridging the infrastructure gap', Centre for Progressive Capitalism, June 2016

12 Madsen Pirie, 'The Fifth Way', Adam Smith Institute, 2017

13 Tim Montgomerie, 'Much of the green belt isn't actually worth protecting – so let's use it now to build vital homes', *The Sun*, 2 February 2017

14 Allister Heath, 'Only a high stakes offer on housing can reopen the door for the Conservatives', *The Daily Telegraph*, 5 June 2017

15 Tim Wallace, 'Homes target may never be met, warns housing guru', *The Daily Telegraph*, 8 October 2017

16 'Forward, Together: Our plan for a Stronger Britain and a Prosperous Future: The Conservative and Unionist Party Manifesto', 2017

17 The full press release can be read here: https://julesbirch.com/2017/05/14/the-conservative-manifesto-plan/

18 Michael Barnes QC, *The Law of Compulsory Purchase and Compensation*, Hart Publishing, 2014, p.175

19 DCLG, 'Consultation on further reform of the compulsory purchase system', September 2016

20 Aubrey, 'Bridging the Infrastructure Gap'